WHAT CAN A PARENT DO?

Handbook for the 'Fives to Fifteens' Basic Parenting Programme
(formerly the Veritas Basic Parenting Programme)

Written by Michael & Terri Quinn in conjunction with community, parent-teacher and church groups throughout Britain & Ireland.

D1439256

FAMILY CARING TRUST

First published 1986
by Veritas Family Resources,
7/8 Lower Abbey Street,
Dublin 1.

Published 1987
by Family Caring Trust,
44 Rathfriland Road,
Newry, Co Down BT34 1LD

Revised editions published 1988 (and 1994)
by Family Caring Trust.
Reprinted 1989, 1990 (twice), 1991, 1992, 1993,
1994 (twice), 1995, 1996, 1997, 1998

Design: Bill Bolger
Illustrations: John Byrne and Pauline McGrath
Printing: Universities Press, (Belfast)

Our thanks to 'Reality' magazine
for permission to reprint the passage
'And more needs...'

ISBN 0 86217 176 8

CONTENTS

Page

FAMILY CARING TRUST

IS PARTICULARLY GRATEFUL TO

FOR THEIR GENEROUS CONTRIBUTION

TOWARDS THE DEVELOPMENT AND PRODUCTION

OF THIS BOOK AND PROGRAMME

CHILDREN HAVE RIGHTS

The UN Convention on the Rights of the Child is the first document to attempt to write down all the rights of children. Here are some highlights - and some corresponding rights of parents. It may help to try replacing 'right to' with 'need (for)' and to think of these rights in terms of basic needs.

1. Children have a right to be respected by their parents or guardians, and to be involved in decisions that affect themselves.
2. Children have a right to say what they want and think and feel so long as doing so does not break the law or affect other people's rights.
3. Children have a right to personal privacy, including not having personal letters opened or phone calls listened to unless the law allows this.
4. Children have a right to a wide range of information, especially any which would make life better for them.
5. Children have a right to proper care and protection from all forms of violence, including cruel punishment, belittling, or lack of respect.
6. Children have a right to an adequate standard of living, good food, good health care, and the best possible chance to develop fully.
7. Disabled children have a right to be enabled to take an active, full part in everyday life and become as independent as possible.
8. Every child is entitled to rest and play, and to have the chance to join in a wide range of activities.

...AND PARENTS HAVE RIGHTS

1. Parents have the same right to be listened to and respected by their children as their children have to be listened to and respected by their parents.
2. Parents have a right to time for relaxing and developing themselves - also a right to time on their own with a spouse or other significant adult.
3. Parents have a right to postpone making a decision until they have had time to think.
4. Parents have a right to say 'no', to set reasonable limits for their children, and, within reason, to let them live with the results of ignoring those limits.
5. Parents have a right to have their work at home valued and appreciated by the significant people in their lives as well as by government and state bodies.
6. Parents have the right to ask their children for reasonable help around the home, according to each child's ability.
7. Parents have a right to communicate their values and opinions to their children - though they cannot insist on their children having the same values.
8. Parents have a right to proper support in providing their children with due rights and respect.

Do you agree that you and your children have these rights? Which of your children's rights might you find hardest to respect? Which of your own rights might you find hardest to claim?

BEFORE YOU START...

This book is part of an eight-week parenting programme, which also includes posters, a Leader's guide and cassette tapes. Parents find the book useful on its own, but it may be important to bear in mind that it is part of a course which parents take just a little at a time. It may be a better idea to read the book a little at a time rather than attempt to read right through it at one sitting.

A book on its own can only do so much - it will make a lot more sense to those who also have the support of a small group of other parents. Such a group can give parents a great sense of not being on their own, and can also help to lessen any feelings of guilt. For the truth is that, given your circumstances, you have always done the best you could for your children. You have never deliberately hurt or harmed them. It is pointless to blame yourself for not doing something that you were not even aware of at the time. Isn't it much better to concentrate on using the opportunities that present themselves today.

If you are interested in belonging to a group, then, you might like to contact your school, parent teacher association, church, or a local organisation that is interested in family life. Family Caring Trust provides ongoing support and the materials for running courses to thousands of such groups.

The aim of this book

Much of our parenting seems to depend on how we *communicate* with our children - not making empty threats; sometimes saying very little, even being silent; encouraging; listening; saying how we feel; talking problems through; keeping the lines open... So the principal aim of this book is to help parents improve the way they communicate with their children. Indeed, many parents claim that better communication has been the key to improved discipline, to getting along better with their children, and to winning their co-operation. When children are respected, they are more liable to show respect.

Who is it for?

This book is for ordinary parents, including those who are single or separated and those whose families are broken or mixed as well as those who are happily married. It is written in simple language - though a number of new terms are introduced and explained at different stages. Many good ideas could have been included but were left out in order to keep the book simple and practical; people generally prefer to deal with just one new idea at a time. Most parents probably do not need very special knowledge of child psychology and the development of children. It is enough if they have some basic understanding of and love for their children - and some skills. But some simple psychological ideas have been introduced, mainly those of Alfred Adler, as developed by Dreikurs, Dinkmeyer and McKay (notably natural and logical consequences, and the goals of misbehaviour). For parents who want more information there is a recommended reading list at the back of the book.

Parents of teenagers tend to find this book as useful as do parents of pre-schoolers. The challenges of an adolescent may be quite different to those of a younger child, but the skills for dealing with them are basically the same. It has even been found helpful to have parents of different age groups do the course together. However, the Teen-Parenting Programme (also available from Family Caring Trust) has been specially developed for parents of teenagers who have done the basic course and who then wish to move on to look at more specific teenage challenges.

Using what works for you.
The suggestions in this book will not be suitable for everyone; many parents are already doing a very good job and are not using these methods. Naturally, it's important to try out the ideas in order to find out what does work for you, but none of these ideas is sacred - each of you is different, your family background is different and your children are different. Parents often find that what works with one child doesn't work with another - or even with the same child at a different time. So there is no one way to bring up children. A great deal depends on your circumstances, on the position of a child in your family - even on your mood. It would be foolish not to listen to experts, of course, but it's not helpful to let experts dictate to you or tell you how to bring up your children. No one knows your children as you do. So feel free to reject or disagree with anything in these pages that does not suit you.

Some examples in the book may seem unusual or extreme - like giving your daughter an alarm clock to get herself up in the morning. But it is important to see an example like this in context. It may not be appropriate in your family. But if you are wearing yourself out every morning coaxing and nagging at a child who lies on in bed, it may be a good idea to give her an alarm clock and allow her to face the consequences of being late for school. Use what works for you.

The examples in the book are taken from many different kinds of family situation and social background. In one family, problems may arise over pocket-money; in another family, parents may not give their children pocket-money at all. In one family there may be tension over a teenager's careless driving of the parents' car; another family may not be able to afford a car and may be experiencing acute problems as a result of un-employment; a third family's problems may arise from the difficulties of bringing up children as a single parent. But when parents see how the principles of this programme apply to a number of different situations, it is usually not difficult to apply them to their own families.

Beliefs and influences
It may be important, right from the start, to acknowledge some of the beliefs and influences affecting our own ideas on bringing up children. We

believe in a balanced approach to parenting - neither rigidly authoritarian nor overly permissive. It is obviously important for parents to recognise that their children have certain basic rights, and this book respects those rights and aims to foster them. But it is also important to recognise that parents have *their* rights too - and these need to be equally respected and fostered if we are to have balanced parenting and a healthy society in the future. Indeed, parents may need to be helped to appreciate their special leadership role in the family, guiding, supporting, stimulating, stretching, encouraging, challenging, listening, setting an example, and generally creating an environment in which children can learn to love, to become responsible and to develop their fullest potential. Our aim in this programme is not to change or modify children's behaviour to come up to some kind of ideal or model behaviour. Each child is a unique and special person, and part of a parent's role is to encourage not only responsibility and co-operation but also creativity and uniqueness in the child.

Acknowledgements

There is little that is original in the book. We owe a great deal to the ideas of Alfred Adler, Don Dinkmeyer, Rudolf Dreikurs, Gerard Egan, Thomas Gordon, Harvey Jackins, Gary McKay, Carl Rogers, and Virginia Satir. Also to a number of existing parenting programmes, notably 'Systematic Training for Effective Parenting'; Parent Effectiveness Training'; and 'Practical Parenting.'

We would like to say a special word of thanks to all the people who helped to test this programme throughout Britain and Ireland, in rural and city communities, in multi-racial groups, in well-to-do suburbs, and in underprivileged areas. It would appear from that testing that we are dealing here with basic human situations where people of every walk of life seem to find common cause and to speak a common language.

We would also like to thank those people whom we consulted at various stages about style and content: John Murphy, Michael Molloy, and Gabrielle Allman. Another very patient - and most willing - person was our secretary, Bernie Magill. And we are especially grateful to our own children who have taught us what a difficult, interesting, challenging, but, above all, enjoyable task it can be to be a parent.

A starting point

A word of consolation to finish with. Parents are notorious for all the guilt they carry around about not 'measuring up', not being perfect. But there is no such thing as a perfect parent, and that is certainly not the ideal offered in this book. What about settling for being a 'good enough' parent? Setting that goal for ourselves may create a healthier attitude and be an important starting point on the road to being more effective.

CHAPTER 1: WHAT IS YOUR CHILD LOOKING FOR?

Jane: Mummy, Peter thumped me!

Mrs Stewart: Peter! (Pause) Peter!!

Peter: What's wrong?

Mrs Stewart: Why did you thump Jane?

Peter: I didn't thump her. She was annoying me, and I pushed her away.

Jane: No, Mummy. I was watching TV and he came in and switched it over to something *he* wanted to see, and he thumped me when I tried to switch it back.

Peter: I didn't thump you, cry-baby! I switched over because I always watch that programme. And you know it, you little b..!

Mrs Stewart: I won't have you using that language in this house, Peter! And I don't know how often I've spoken to you about bullying. I'll kill you one of these days if you don't stop it!

Peter: Sure, blame me! I always get the blame. But little 'angel-face' never does anything wrong! Well, I'm just fed-up with all the blame! (Peter goes out, and slams the door.)

Mrs Stewart: (rushes to door) Peter! Come back in here again, and walk out through this door properly! That's no way to treat...

How we take the bait

This kind of scene is not uncommon in many families. Squabbling among children can be discouraging and very upsetting for parents, and they are often at a loss to know what to do.

But what do you think of the way Mrs Stewart was handling the situation? She's not being very effective, is she? - the squabbling, the bullying and the tattling are obviously problems that keep cropping up again and again in her family. And did you notice how she took her children's bait? - first Jane's, and then Peter's. Her children probably know exactly what she's going to say, for she keeps letting herself get drawn into blaming, scolding, making empty threats, and attempting to correct on the spot. She is doing her best to be a good parent, but she tends to act in a fixed, patterned, unthinking - and ineffective - way.

The fact is that most children know exactly how to get their parents' attention. They are experts at drawing us into their problems and their squabbles. It's like pressing a button - they can get us to nag,

9

coax, scold, lecture, shout, threaten, hit - even to look for their lost belongings and do things for them that they are quite capable of doing for themselves! Countless times every day, a great many parents take their children's bait and get hooked into situations like the one above! These parents *reward* their children's misbehaviour, even reinforce it, by paying so much attention to it (by misbehaviour we mean any behaviour which does not respect self or others). Even if the misbehaviour stops for a few minutes, it is almost certain to start again the next time the child wants attention - as long as we parents do just what our children expect us to do.

Why do children misbehave?

But what exactly are children seeking when they misbehave? Why do they misbehave in the first place?

Children usually misbehave because they feel bad about themselves, because they feel discouraged. That is not surprising when you think of how much they have to learn and accomplish in the first few years of their lives. When they feel discouraged at not achieving something, they fall back, frustrated, to an earlier stage and seek help in the only way they know - they express their fears, loneliness, worries, doubts and discouragement in 'troublesome' behaviour. Here are five common ways in which this behaviour is expressed:

1. Attention-seeking (keeping people busy with them).
2. Power contests (trying to run things).
3. Revenge (trying to hurt people).
4. Showing inadequacy (giving up).
5. Seeking the approval of friends (closely linked to attention-seeking.)

We'll look at some examples of these five ways, and how parents might begin to deal with them.

Attention-seeking

Two year old John gets attention by dropping food on the floor. When his mother says: 'Stop that,' he stops, but, one minute later, he's at it again. Mother is giving him the attention he is looking for.

Attention-seeking is very common. Some children want attention so desperately that they prefer to be punished or scolded or to do without food rather than be ignored. Watch what happens when you give attention on demand - the misbehaviour may stop for a while, but it is likely to be repeated soon again - or the child misbehaves in another way.

A misbehaviour tends to stop when it is not being rewarded, for example when it is not being noticed, when it is being ignored. So it is best not to give attention on demand to a misbehaving child, at least not to do what the child *expects* you to do. But John's mother still needs to give him attention, cuddles, stories, play - when he is *not* expecting it.

Power contests

Eleven year-old Mary becomes defiant when she is asked to do something. When her father insists, there are angry scenes and the whole atmosphere of the house is affected.

This is probably a power struggle. When children who seek power are corrected, they often ignore the correction - or get worse. Even when they give in, they may remain defiant.

It is usually better not to try to win power contests. For 'winning' often makes matters worse in the long run. Mary's father can refuse to get involved in the power struggle. Instead, he can leave the room saying: 'We'll talk about this later, Mary, when we're both calmer.' But it's important to remember to talk about it later!

Revenge

Eight year old Liz punishes her parents by constantly complaining about the 'rotten old food' they give her. When she is forbidden to speak like that, she mutters under her breath and makes mealtimes a kind of torture for her parents. She has found an effective way of getting her own back. Without even realising it, she may be seeking revenge.

When parents win power struggles regularly, children may seek revenge by finding ways to hurt and punish them. Parents are tempted to hit back, scold, nag - all to no avail. The child merely changes tactics and finds a new way to hurt. So it is not helpful to fight back.

This kind of situation is difficult. If you remain friendly, however, you'll soon take the bitterness out of the 'war.' In this case, it may be better to acknowledge calmly that Liz does not like the food and ask her to leave the table if she doesn't want to eat it - then you might change the subject.

Showing inadequacy

Five year old Sean dilly-dallies over dressing himself and cannot 'work the buttons.' Morning after morning, Sean's mother takes the bait - first she nags at him, and then she comes to his rescue. Sean is getting all the attention he wants by showing inadequacy, although he has come no nearer to learning to 'work the buttons.'

Discouraged children sometimes show such inadequacy that parents will often end up either criticising them or coming to their aid, or drawing attention to the inadequacy. This obviously makes matters worse, for such children may then feel more incapable and inadequate than ever. So there is no improvement.

The first step in dealing with 'inadequate' children is to stop rewarding the inadequacy by criticising it - even by noticing it. The other thing that helps a lot is to look for some little improvement to encourage - even an *effort* at improvement.

Approval of friends

Fifteen year old Trevor stays out late with his friends. In spite of his mother's scolding and lecturing, his time-keeping shows no improvement.

As children get older, it becomes more and more important to them to impress their friends. This can lead to misbehaviour that worries or frightens parents. As a result, parents can easily fall into a pattern of lecturing and disapproving.

If Trevor's mother scolds him in front of his friends, he will feel hurt and angry, and may become more hostile. She might do better to postpone dealing with the problem for the moment and to take an interest in what he has been doing with his friends. Later, she will be able to deal with the issue more effectively - as we will see in the chapter on discipline.

Changing our approach

These, then, are some of the main reasons why children misbehave - to gain attention, power, revenge, to show inadequacy, to win the approval of friends... Children, of course, don't do these things consciously; they usually misbehave without knowing what they are seeking.

When a child misbehaves, it helps to ask: 'How am I feeling right now?' For my feelings are often a clue to which of the five things my child is looking for. When I feel *annoyed*, the child is probably seeking *attention*; when I'm *angry*, the child's goal is probably *power*; when I feel *hurt*, that tells me that the child is probably seeking *revenge*; a *helpless* feeling is usually a sign that the child is showing *inadequacy*; and when I feel *worried* or *alarmed*, my child may be seeking the *approval of friends*. Once the child's goal is clear, I can avoid the bait by not reacting in my usual way. Many people see that as the first step to becoming a more effective parent.

The suggestion, then, is that you do the unexpected, perhaps the exact opposite to what you normally do. If you normally shout, try being quiet. If you're normally quiet, try asserting yourself. Refuse to give attention on demand. Back off when you find yourself getting hooked into an argument or a fight. Look for something to encourage when you feel like criticising. Ignore fighting and squabbling unless there is real danger. In this way you can begin to change unthinking patterns of parenting that are not effective, and you will no longer be rewarding misbehaviour.

Time together

In this course, there is a lot of emphasis on skills for dealing with children, but it is more than a question of mere skills - our main task and duty as parents is to love our children. And that demands time. Time to talk together. Time to listen. Time to show affection, to relax and laugh together. Time to encourage. Time to play. Time to have fun together. Time to relax over a meal together. Giving positive attention to children may also be one of the most effective and powerful ways of doing the opposite to what we normally do.

GETTING IN TOUCH

Which of the following behaviours upset you in any of your children? Feel free to tick any that upset you. Are there other behaviours you'd like to add to the list?

Won't get up in the mornings. Doesn't dress/ wash properly. Won't wash without being reminded. Leaves door open. Messes food. Has bad table manners. Answers back. Constantly fighting and squabbling. Throws tantrums. Moans and complains. Is very slow. Rushes meals. Neglects or rushes homework. Uncooperative at home. Watches too much TV. Bullies. Tells lies. Doesn't communicate. Won't go to bed on time. Won't stay in bed when settled. Shows lack of respect for others. Neglects pet dog or cat. Doesn't mix - no friends. Climbs on furniture. Writes on walls. Throws tantrums. Comes late for meals. Moody and depressed. Stays out too late. Something else?...

B. What do you normally do when this behaviour upsets you? - smack, scold, ignore the misbehaviour, remove the child, deprive the child of a treat, threaten, plead, promise rewards... What would you like to do instead? Can you think of anything that might work better?

 # PLANS FOR NEXT WEEK

As well as reading chapter two, the suggestion for next week is that we think of one example of misbehaviour that is ongoing (i.e., where we are not being effective), and then plan to do the unexpected, perhaps the opposite to what we usually do. There is no guarantee that this will work, but it *probably* will - and we have nothing to lose anyway if we are not being effective at present! The more specific we are in planning what we will do, the better. It may help to write down what exactly we plan to do. (Who with? When? Where?..)

Plans..._____

TABLE 1: AVOIDING THE BAIT

The table below* sums up some of the main points in Chapter 1. Does it help you to see ways in which you could be more effective?

BAIT	PARENT SEES BAIT	AND GETS HOOKED IN	AVOIDING THE BAIT
Constant squabbling and fighting between Sarah and John. Loud screams and regular complaints to get mother's attention.	When child seeks ATTENTION parent usually feels ANNOYED.	Mother rewards this behaviour by paying attention to it - trying to sort out fights, correcting, reminding, scolding... But misbehaviour soon continues. Her method is not effective.	Try to avoid getting involved in children's squabbles unless there is real danger. Refuse to give attention on demand. But make time for positive attention when it is not expected.
11 year old Mike refuses point-blank to clear his dishes off the table or help with the washing-up.	When child enters POWER contest, parent may feel ANGRY.	Mike's father lectures, argues, then forces his son to obey. Mike hates father and secretly plots revenge.	It is usually more effective not to seek to win power struggles. Pull out of the fight and talk it out later, when everyone is calmer.
17 year old Marie has refused to speak to her father for three weeks.	When child seeks REVENGE parent may feel VERY HURT.	Father rants and raves about what will happen if she continues to refuse to speak to him. She becomes more entrenched and bitter.	It's unhelpful to play the retaliation game with your children. When you stay friendly and cheerful, the atmosphere will gradually improve.
8 year old George is slow and awkward - and has no friends.	When child shows INADEQUACY, parent may feel HOPELESS/ HELPLESS.	George's parents some-times coax, sometimes nag, sometimes give up on him. They often take pity on him and take over his tasks. George shows no improvement.	Neither pity nor criticism is helpful. Keep on the lookout for efforts or improvements and 'notice' them. Encouragement works wonders.
13 year old Evelyn has lost interest in studying and has began to stay out later and later in the evenings.	When child seeks APPROVAL of FRIENDS parents may feel WORRIED/ ANXIOUS.	Evelyn's parents scold, nag and threaten. There are constant rows and bad feelings. The atmosphere in the house is depressing and unpleasant.	Try showing interest in Evelyn and her friends and make time for chats with her. For more serious problems action may be more effective than talking - see chapter 6.

* This Table is based on the discoveries and thinking of Alfred Adler as developed by Rudolf Dreikurs. Don Dinkmeyer and Gary McKay.

 # CASE STUDIES

(Alternative to listening to the audio tapes)

Read the following conversations (it's more fun if two or three people read them aloud). Then, in groups of three, discuss the questions at the end of each situation.

MOTHER: (annoyed) Jim, what have I said to you about dumping your schoolbag in the front room! And look where you've thrown your jacket!
JIM: (crossly) I'll pick them up in a minute.
NARRATOR: Half an hour later...
MOTHER: (angrily) Hey, I thought you were going to take these things out of the room!
JIM: Aw, get off my back. I told you I was going to do it. Give me a chance, will you!
MOTHER: (angrily) Look, if you don't pick up your bag and your jacket and get them out of here quickly, I'll... I'll... You'll see what'll happen to you! Now I'm warning you!
NARRATOR: Eventually, after more nagging and threatening, Jim removed his belongings - though he proceeded to dump his schoolbag in the passageway outside his bedroom.

By the end of this situation, the mother is angry - and we see from Table 1 that anger is a clue that she may be getting locked into a power struggle - but can you see ways in which she is being ineffective, even rewarding Jim's behaviour?

FATHER: What are you two doing out of bed? Get back up those stairs !
JANE: But Dad, Sonya pulled my hair.
FATHER: Sonya! Did you? Did you pull her hair?
SONYA: I didn't mean to pull it.
JANE: Yes, you did!
SONYA: No, I didn't... Anyway, you were singing and you wouldn't let me get to sleep!
FATHER: (annoyed) I don't know which of you is the worst! But Sonya, you're older and you ought to know better!... Now, up the stairs this instant, and if there's another sound from either of you, I'll go up and smack you!

Father is annoyed in this situation - a clue that his children may be seeking attention. How is he being ineffective - and actually rewarding the squabbling?

GARY: (Giggling with his friend, Clive). Huh, I've spilt my milk. (More giggles).
MOTHER: (annoyed) Now look what you've done! What's come over you this evening, Gary? You usually behave yourself at the table!
GARY: (desperate to impress Clive) No I don't! These stupid glasses are too easy to knock over anyway.
MOTHER: (angry) Gary, don't talk to me like that. I won't have it.
GARY: (mimicking) 'I won't have it! I won't have it!' (More giggles).
MOTHER: (angrily) Go to your bedroom this instant!
GARY: Good. I don't want your stinking food. Coming, Clive?

Why do you think Gary is acting like this? And how is his mother being ineffective?

TIPS FOR PARENTS

When children feel bad about themselves, they cannot think clearly; they try to get attention, power, etc., in the hope that this will make them feel good again. But try not to take that bait! It won't make them happy; you may only reward the misbehaviour and reinforce it! Try doing the unexpected instead, the opposite to what you normally do. (Ignore the tantrums or the squabbling, back off, leave the room for a while...) That will change the rules of the game and you'll soon see a change for the better. It's also important to encourage positive behaviour too, by giving time, attention or encouragement to the child later - as soon as you can.

Many of us tend to treat our children in rigid, patterned, unthinking ways. It's not easy to change these patterns of a lifetime. So just aim for a little change at a time. Forget about being a very good parent for the time being - think of just one situation where you're not being effective, perhaps with one child, and just aim at *not* doing what you usually do. That can be a good start!

Four pillars of good relationships are:
l. Respect for one other (I respect myself and you - so I will not let you walk over me. This includes communicating to you that others matter as much as us).
2. Encouragement (See chapter three).

3. Time for fun (fun is great for lightening a situation and winning co-operation).
4. Love (Shared with all family members - I need to communicate regularly to my children that they matter, that I like them). It helps a lot to make time for giving positive attention to your children, if necessary by planning outings, fun-times, a relaxed meal-time. These all help to build a relaxed loving atmosphere which can be so good for children's growth and development.

Recent research shows that the children of single parents are not necessarily at a disadvantage - they often turn out more mature and balanced than other children because of the extra time the parent tends to spend with them. Other research shows that children who grow up in a home where two parents love each other also have a head-start in life. So it would appear to be important for parents, when possible, to spend a good deal of time both together and with their children.

If you are at home with a child all day, you need a break. Try to arrange to have at least half an hour every day for quiet time. During that quiet time, it usually helps to be lying down with your feet off the ground. Remember it's not just for your own sake - you owe it to your child!

Hitting, slapping, beating, putting down, in fact power struggles and violence of any kind, tend to create further violence and the desire for revenge. Society will hardly change until the family changes. That's how important your approach can be.

Don't be afraid to ignore misbehaviour at times. You may actually be rewarding that behaviour by paying attention to it - for example if you are correcting your four year old son again and again for using swear words. Ignoring is not the same as approving - it can be sobering!

CHAPTER 2: BECOMING A RESPONSIBLE PARENT

Four year old Tom cannot dress himself. Every morning his mother keeps telling him to start dressing, then makes empty threats about what will happen if he does not make an effort - and then scolds him crossly as she dresses him herself. Tom has learnt how good it is to be helpless - he gets so much attention from mother and gets dressed into the bargain. Instead of taking time to train Tom to dress himself, his mother is actually training him not to be responsible for himself. She does not realise this, of course.

Twelve year old Jane is not expected to do any chores at home. Her mother cooks, clears up after meals, washes her clothes, irons them - even makes Jane's bed and tidies her room. 'I don't mind,' her mother says 'I don't want to spoil her childhood on her. And I love my children - I wouldn't like them to go through what I went through when I was a little girl.' Jane's mother would be shocked if someone pointed out to her that she was actually helping Jane to be irresponsible.

Looking at ourselves.
In both of the examples above, the parents are well-meaning but they are drifting along, acting in a patterned, unthinking way, and the result is the opposite to what they want. Their children are not becoming responsible. They may be spending themselves for their children, doing everything they think good parents ought to do. But they do not seem to be asking the very important question: 'What will help my children to become mature and responsible?'

If parents want their children to become responsible, they may need to start by looking at themselves - at their *own* outlook and their *own* behaviour. Take sex roles, for example. Children learn a great deal about the roles of men and women from the way their parents behave - and from what their parents expect of them. Think about how different a boy's training for life is when he is expected to cook, clean, sew, etc. - and when he sees his father doing some household chores. Older

16

primary school children, boys as well as girls, can be taught to iron their own clothes - and expected to do so!

Occasionally, some parents of teenagers think: 'But it's too late now for me to change!' It is never too late to change. That is the most important point Virginia Satir makes in her book 'Peoplemaking.' No matter how bad the situation in your family is, no matter how hopeless it may appear, there is always hope. Change is always possible - in every important aspect of family life. That is not theory; it comes out of a great deal of experience.

Being a 'good' parent.

In what ways can a parent change? One of the major changes that this course encourages is to stop being a 'good' parent and become instead a responsible parent.

'Good' parents try to do everything for their children. They become like servants. They remind and coax their children, they pick up their clothes, make their school lunches, help with dressing them, supervise their eating, settle their fights, etc., etc.

In spite of all their good intentions, these 'good' parents may be harming their children. If they take upon themselves their children's responsibilities, they may leave the children over-dependent (or rebellious). If their children are not allowed to learn form experience or from the consequences of their actions; they may grow up lacking in confidence because so many choices are made for them.

Being a responsible parent.

An alternative to being a 'good' parent is to be a *responsible* parent. Responsible parents treat their children with equality and respect and they encourage them as far as possible to make their own decisions - and to live with the consequences. 'Good' parents may not be showing that respect to their children. And they are not respecting *themselves* when they allow their children to treat them as servants.

For children become remarkably responsible when they are given responsibility. Seven year old children can make

their own school lunches; children of all ages can settle their own fights; teenagers can have their own alarm-clocks and take responsibility for getting themselves up in the morning - or face the consequences of being late for school. All that saves a lot of wear and tear on parents. And it is a more effective and responsible approach.

Responsible parents are firm but not controlling. They respect their children's rights and expect to be given theirs. For example, if the children are playing very noisily in the kitchen, mother can say: 'I'm sorry, I'm afraid the noise is too much for me. You can do something quietly in the kitchen or you can make as much noise as you like playing outside or in the bedroom. Which do you want to do?' With this calm approach, mother is claiming her own rights and respecting the children's right to choose.

Or take the case of Paul who is always 'losing' things. As long as he has 'good' parents who keep finding his missing shoes, toys, etc., for him, he may never learn to care about his own belongings. When he has to live with the consequences of his carelessness, however, he can begin to become more responsible.

The responsible parent's approach also *works* much better than nagging, forbidding or taking away a child's freedom to choose. It helps children to grow in maturity by building their self-confidence and their sense of responsibility. And it also makes for a real growth in children's conscience as they are encouraged, supported and challenged in making their own choices.

The need for training and guidance.

Now, there is a common misunderstanding here. Giving children responsibilities is not meant to be a lazy way out for parents. 'Latch-key kids' are also given responsibility - too much responsibility - with no supervision, no support, no guiding hand. Parents can start right away to give their children more responsibilities, but these should be given gradually, in stages. It is essential to set aside time for *training* a child.

Unfortunately, a parent can sometimes be quite happy as long as the children are not being a nuisance - although they may be spending hours on end in front of the television or moping in a bedroom. It can be important, then, to stretch and stimulate children in order to develop responsibility and creativity in them. Attempts to stretch them may meet with hostility at first, but they will soon get engrossed in the new situation - painting, reading, gardening or whatever.

As children take on new tasks, a parent can be beside them, their best friend, present to them, encouraging them, asking questions, showing and helping when necessary, letting them try for themselves and gradually withdrawing into the background, pleased to see them making an effort, improving, growing. At times parents can be close by as their children draw, paint, play, create, experiment, explore, discover... They can be with their children as the children learn to dress themselves, to wash their teeth, to tie their shoes, to cross the road, to ride a bicycle, to wash their own hair, to cook, to bake, to play the guitar, to tackle new school work, to wash and dry the dishes, to vacuum, to sew. It does not matter if the parents cannot understand the schoolwork or play the guitar themselves - these are not merely opportunities to develop responsibility in children but to encourage them and to build a bond with them. With a parent beside them a new challenge can be fun.

GETTING IN TOUCH

Here are some things parents do for their children - which their children (depending on their ages) might do for themselves. Study the list and tick off anything you do which you think your children might be capable of doing. If you have time, you might ask yourself at what age children would be capable of each of these responsibilities.

Get them up in the mornings;
Dress their beds; tidy their rooms;
Choose and lay out their clothes for the following day;
Dress them; tie their shoes;
Dress the baby;
Choose and buy their clothes;
Make school lunches; prepare breakfast; cook; prepare their meals;
Pick up their clothes; tidy away their toys;
Bath them; wash faces; brush teeth; wash their hair; comb hair;
Supervise their eating;
Iron their clothes; sew; knit;
Lay the table and clear it;
Sweep the kitchen floor; dust the house; vacuum the floor;
Clean and tidy the bathroom; clean windows;
Sort out and fold newly-washed clothes;
Settle fights and squabbles;
Go to the post office/ shop;
Do all their homework with them;
Clean the car; change the oil; drive the car;
Paint inside and outside the house;
Mow the lawn; dig the garden; plant flowers and vegetables;
Make up prayers; lead prayers;
Mend bicycle punctures;
Wire an electric plug; change a fuse;
Use saw/hammer; chop firewood;
Make the decisions about their routines, their friends, their lifestyle, their future.

PLANS FOR NEXT WEEK

What are you doing for your children that they could do for themselves? What new responsibilities could you begin to introduce them to during the next week? Be as specific as possible - who? what? when? how will you start? You may like to write your plans...

Plans..._____

_____

TABLE 2 - WHICH KIND OF PARENT?

Parents are asked to consider the two types of parent in the table below. Do you think the parents' behaviour does have the effects shown in the second and fourth columns?

'GOOD' PARENT TYPES		PARENTS WHO DEVELOP RESPONSIBILITY	
Behaviour	**Effect**	**Behaviour**	**Effect**
1. Controls by punishment or by rewards. Is always right. Expects obedience and has to win.	Child fights back or gives up. Becomes dishonest, tells lies. Doesn't learn self-control.	Parent allows child to make decisions. Positive and encouraging.	Child grows in confidence. Learns decision-making.
2. Wants perfection. Finds fault constantly. Needs child to behave so neighbours will approve.	Child becomes discouraged - can't measure up. May try to be 'perfect.' Over-anxious about pleasing.	Parent is happy with small improvements and encourages child's strengths.	Child gains belief in self. Becomes more willing to 'have a go.'
3. Suspicious. Doesn't trust child. Hedges child in with rules and regulations.	Child feels guilty. Distrusts others.	Parent trusts child and looks for efforts to encourage.	Child grows in freedom and belief in self. Learns to trust others.
4. Feels superior and takes over child's responsibilities. Over-protective, pities, shames, spoils.	Child feels helpless. Expects others to do everything.	Parent shows respect for child and encourages responsibility.	Child learns self-respect. Becomes more responsible.
5. Cannot say no. Constantly gives in to child. Becomes doormat.	Child becomes 'spoilt' and selfish. Can't make friends. Greedy.	Parent is firm. Respects own rights and child's rights. Encourages co-operation.	Child learns to co-operate. Makes friends easily.

CASE STUDIES

(Alternative to listening to the audio tapes)

Read the following conversations (it may be better if two or three people read them aloud). Then, in groups of three, discuss the questions at the end of each conversation.

JILL (15): Dad, would you drive me down to the swimming pool? I need to be there for seven.

FATHER: Look, Jill, this is becoming a habit! I'm in the middle of something now and I can't leave it. Why didn't you think of going earlier and you could have taken your bike?

JILL: Well, I just forgot, and I'm going to be late if you don't take me (almost in tears). Please, Dad, will you?

FATHER: (With a sigh) All right, I'll do it this time, but you really ought to think ahead.

Parents need to be available for genuine emergencies - but not for regularly occurring 'emergencies' that could have been foreseen and that are the result of carelessness or forgetfulness. In what ways was this father a 'good' parent rather than a responsible one? What could he have done instead to encourage responsibility in Jill?

FATHER: Patricia! What are you at? You're slobbering your food there like a little pig... (pause) Patricia! Did you hear what I said to you? It's disgusting to sit here and watch you! Use your spoon... No, not that hand, the other hand... Hold it steady. Steady! Aaah! Now look what you've done, stupid! Quick! Someone get a cloth and wipe it up!

In what ways is the father not encouraging Patricia to be responsible? What might he have done instead to help her learn better table-manners?

MOTHER (speaking to nine year old son): Come on, John, it's your bedtime.... Quickly. Look at the time. You know I shouldn't have to remind you night after night!...
(Two minutes later...) John! I said it's bedtime. Now that's it! Come on, your supper's on the table five minutes... That's it, now, drink it up... Now your teeth... Where's your toothbrush?... Aw, come on now, this is crazy. You know where you're supposed to keep your toothbrush... Here it is. Now don't be a minute - I'll get your pyjamas... Have you been to the toilet?...

In what ways was the mother a 'good' parent rather than a responsible one? What could she have done instead to encourage responsibility in John?

TIPS FOR PARENTS

Encourage and train your son to cook , sew, iron and do household tasks - and help your daughter to use a screwdriver, to change an electric plug, to dig the garden... Your own *example* as parents is an important part of that training.

One of the best ways to help people become responsible is to *give* them responsibility. Ask yourself: 'What am I doing that my children could do for themselves?' Then plan to involve them gradually.

Giving increased responsibility to children will result in less tension between you and them and it will take some of the burden off your shoulders. But that is not the main reason for it. The chief purpose is to help them grow into responsible caring, co-operative individuals themselves.

Developing responsibility does not just mean handing over more *tasks* to your children. It also includes giving them increasing freedom to make their *own* decisions, to choose what they will wear and eat and buy and how they will spend their time. But this responsibility should not be handed over without spending time training, showing, encouraging, supporting - and continuing to challenge their behaviour. It is good to begin that process *now* rather than postpone it.

Don't suddenly expect children to take on new responsibilities. Spend time with them training, showing, encouraging. Make the new task enjoyable - even fun, if possible - and help the child see it as a grown-up, responsible, co-operative thing to do. Continue to support the child for as long as necessary (and try never to take the contribution completely for granted). Many parents find the following five steps helpful:

   1. Tell them what to do.
   2. Show them.
   3. Let them try.
   4. Observe - and occasionally check how things are going.
   5. Keep encouraging progress.

You can also encourage responsibility in your children by your own example of being responsible - your discipline in eating and drinking, your not listening to scandal, your honesty, your married love, your caring for neighbours...

It may be a good idea to consider giving your children a weekly money allowance instead of money for school-snacks, treats, discos, etc. That can help to make them responsible for balancing their own budgets.

Becoming a responsible parent rather than a 'good' parent does not mean becoming less caring. Warmth, caring and affection are essential. This is not necessarily a question of hugging and kissing, of course - it may just mean staying in there with a child, continuing to care even when things are very difficult. Try to be warm and affectionate in applying new ideas - not cold or clinical. Similarly, it is not enough just to say 'Settle your own squabbles.' You may need to sit down with your children from time to time to talk out ways of dealing non-violently with conflict.

CHAPTER 3: ENCOURAGEMENT

Jane, (twelve) and Teresa (fourteen), have just received their school reports. Jane comes rushing to her mother to show her how well she has done.

Mother: 'This is wonderful, dear. And look at your maths. Ninety two! It's fantastic. Wait 'till your father sees this. He'll be so proud! But what about Teresa. Where is she?

Jane: Oh, you know her. She's stupid. She just threw her report on the floor.

Mother: What? Teresa! Come here this minute. And bring me your report, miss!

Teresa: (Handing over report) You won't like it.

Mother (Reading): I certainly don't. My God! - look at you geography. This is a disgrace. You've made no effort. Why can't you work like Jane instead of letting us all down like this! Honestly. I don't know what's going to become of you!

In this incident, Teresa is already a discouraged child. Her mother is adding to her discouragement with her comments. She expects little of her, she criticises her and she compares her to her younger sister - all ways of discouraging. What is not so obvious is that mother may also be discouraging *Jane* too. For praise, as we will see, often discourages children from making their own decisions and makes them over dependant on what their parents think of them.

How parents discourage children

In many homes, parents try to improve their children by concentrating on the children's mistakes. They criticise, punish, nag, scold, shame, boss... They are expert at finding fault. That is so discouraging to a child. Parents also discourage by taking over and doing their children's tasks or by making all kinds of decisions for their children - giving them the message that they are not capable of doing the tasks or making the decisions themselves.

Let's look at some other ways we can discourage children. Are our standards too high? Do we expect our children's rooms, clothes, homework, household tasks to be neat and perfect? Is what we expect reasonable for their ages? Do we praise a successful child in front of a less successful one? When we compare one child with another we often encourage competition instead of co-operation. And competition almost always discourages the weaker child.

Do we have one set of standards for ourselves and a different one for our children? Do we keep our own bedrooms as tidy as we expect the children to keep theirs? Do we feel free to interrupt our children but insist that they must not interrupt us? Treating children as inferiors in this way discourages them.

Look out for positive behaviour.

Our society does not train us to encourage, but when we are on the lookout for effort and improvement, children begin to grow in confidence and make great strides. 'You got 10 out of 20 right' is so much more helpful a comment than: 'You got 10 out of 20 wrong.' It helps to look on the positive side, to be happy with *effort* - one step at a time - rather than to look for success or final results. With daily practice, this is a skill any parent can learn.

Now, children's behaviour needs to be *corrected, so w*hat happens when a child's behaviour causes problems and cannot be ignored? It is important, first of all, to separate the deed from the doer. Better to correct the deed but not to criticise the person. For example, Marion can be asked to wipe up the milk she has spilt - but should not be told she is clumsy or careless. Bart can be told it is wrong to hit the baby but he should not be told he himself is 'bold' or naughty or bad. As it progresses, this course aims to give parents skills in correcting misbehaviour without criticising the person.

When possible it is better to ignore misbehaviour and concentrate instead on noticing positive behaviour. For example, children's squabbles and fights can be ignored as long as they are not dangerous - children often use such misbehaviour merely to gain your attention. And it is best not to listen to children telling tales on each other. Life will be a lot simpler when they get the message that you are not interested in finding culprits or listening to tattling. It helps to keep on the lookout for something

to encourage, to look for efforts, examples of co-operation, little improvements, talents... Brenda may not be good at washing dishes, but she may be great at clearing the table after meals. Notice her talent and her contribution.

Encouragement is best when it comes from the heart, from having an attitude of thankfulness and gratitude. Many people find it helps them to meditate or take some quiet time every day to become aware of their own goodness and the goodness of others. This attitude of genuine appreciation of others can ensure that our encouragement is more sincere and effective.

The difference between praise and encouragement

Praise is not the same as encouragement. Praise gives *my* judgement of my children's behaviour - which may not help them to believe in themselves. There are times when praise may be quite appropriate, but it is good to be on our guard against its possible bad effects. Praise often discourages. It tends to be given to the child who is good, or great, or who has won - rather than for effort or for a little improvement. Praise tends to compare the child praised to others. Praise can make a child over-anxious about the good opinion of others - instead of encouraging self-assurance. Sometimes, too, praise can be a form of flattery - insincere and unhelpful.

Here are some examples of praise. 'You're great!'; 'You're a very good girl!'; 'You won! That's terrific!'; 'You've behaved very well. I'm proud of you!' In all of these cases, the parents are putting forward their *own* judgements. The children are not being encouraged to judge their own behaviour. Sometimes, of course, these comments may be okay, particularly when a child has gained some genuine success or achievement. But even then we must be careful not to overdo praise, to exaggerate or to compare the child to others. The real test is to ask: 'Are my comments encouraging the child to be more confident and self-assured, to have more belief in herself as a person, to be more at ease with himself?' Praise may not have this effect.

Here are some ways of encouraging without praising:

1. Make a *personal* statement: 'I like...' 'I appreciate...' 'That helps me...' Instead of: 'You're a terrific worker' 'You're better than...' Children can cope with your honest reaction to what they do; but they may be embarrassed or unable to cope with a judgement that they cannot live up to.

2. *Show confidence* in your children's ability. 'I was surprised when you cut the grass last week - it was quite long. I know you'll be able to manage now.' But not: 'You're great for your age' or 'Your drawing is excellent.' In other words, let the children draw their own conclusions about their abilities. It can be encouraging to ask: 'What do you think yourself?' and to allow children the freedom to make up their own minds about their abilities.

3. Focus on the *difficulties* of what your child has done. 'That ground was so hard!' rather than 'You're so strong to have dug that!' Let them fill in the details themselves.

4. Notice *improvement* and *effort*. 'A month ago, you could only swim two lengths.' 'You've spent a full hour working at that.' 'I notice you're getting along much better with Bill recently.' The world we live in puts a great deal of emphasis on success and achievement rather than on effort. So children can easily become discouraged without your support and encouragement for their *efforts*. But try not to spoil it all by adding a comment about how much more they are capable of doing.

5. Keep on the lookout for *contributions*. Since one of our goals in the family is to have co-operation rather than competition, try to keep an eye open for thoughtfulness, consideration or helpfulness. Noticing that with a simple 'Thanks'; 'Thanks for your help'; 'I appreciate what you did for Jane' - even saying 'I need help with...' - can be much more encouraging to a child than saying 'You're very thoughtful/ helpful...'

6. Emphasise the good *effects* of what your child did. 'That makes my work easier' or 'The room looks a lot tidier,' are encouraging remarks because the child knows they are true.

Summing up

To sum up. Try to emphasise the effort, the improvement, the effect, the contribution, the difficulty, in what your children do. Keep your reactions honest and real, and help your children to appreciate for *themselves* the good in what they are doing. Remember that the good is there; we are just not used to looking for it. And when you reflect it back, that can be a great help to your children's growth in confidence.

GETTING IN TOUCH

How often do you make these (or similar) remarks. Put a tick for each statement in the appropriate column.

	Never	Sometimes	Often

DISCOURAGEMENT

Why can't you be like ...
Nag, nag, nag ...
You're a cheeky brat!
Just look at your room, you filthy ...
Don't ... Don't... Don't
You're a very naughty (bold) girl!

PRAISE

What a beautiful picture!
You're terrific!
You look so wonderful!
You're such a good boy!

ENCOURAGEMENT

Thank you. That helps me.
So that's how you do it!
Congratulations. You've improved.
Will you help me with...

PLANS FOR NEXT WEEK

Who is your most discouraged child? In what ways can you encourage that child during the next week? Possibilities include: Being on the lookout for efforts and improvements and 'noticing' them ; trusting them with more responsibilities; saying 'thanks', 'please', 'sorry' and generally showing respect; spending more time with them, especially time listening to them; being cheerful and good-humoured yourself; being interested in them and in their world... You may like to write down your plans.

Plans... _____

_____

TABLE 3: ENCOURAGEMENT

*Below are eight types of parent who often discourage, and eight corresponding types who usually encourage. Can you see yourself in some of them? What have **you** found helps to make children happier and build their confidence and belief in themselves?*

DISCOURAGING PARENT	TYPICAL REMARKS	ENCOURAGING PARENT	TYPICAL REMARKS
1. Looks for success rather than effort.	'You got five wrong out of ten. You'll have to do better than that!'	Looks for little efforts rather than success. Relaxed and accepting.'	'You got five right out of ten. Well done. I notice you're making a greater effort recently.'
2. Wants achievements rather than improvements. Compares child to others.	'Look at Andrew how well he can do it! You're just wasting my time as well as your own!'	Happy with small improvements rather than big achievements.	'That's it. Now you're getting the hang of it!'
3. Does too much for children; becomes their servant.	'I'll find your shoe when I've combed your hair - just be patient.'	Develops responsibility. Allows child to experiment and make mistakes.	'Now, add in the eggs and see what happens...'
4. Takes bait and reacts to child; authoritarian.	'Shut up and get out - and don't you dare talk to me like that again!'	Listens and shows interest in child.	'I see. So it's been very hard for you this week...'
5. Impersonal; often insincere; praises.	'You're absolutely gorgeous. Everyone will love you!'	Makes personal statements; sincere.	'I like that dress on you - it brings out the colour of your eyes.
6. Consoles, reassures, advises.	'Of course you did the right thing, dear - you always do.'	Listens. Allows child to judge for self.	'So what do you think yourself? How do you feel now about what you did?'
7. Threatens, gives orders, scolds, controls, reminds.	'Come on! Get up to your bed this instant or I'll...' (for fifth time)	Encourages child to make own decisions and live with the consequences.	'Oh well. We all make mistakes ... What can you learn from it all?'
8. Criticises; looks out for and points out mistakes.	'Now look what you've done! Why do you have to be so stupid?'	Looks out for positive; is generally good-humoured.	'Oops! Now look what we've done! I'm glad you're with me, or I'd be stuck!'

CASE STUDIES

(Alternative to listening to the audio tapes)

Read the following conversations (it may be better if two or three people read them aloud). Then, in groups of three, discuss the questions at the end of each situation.

Fifteen year old Gwen is very anxious. She's afraid she'll fail her exam next week.

What unhelpful things do parents often do or say in a situation like this? What could her parents do or say, or what questions might they ask - avoiding criticism and avoiding exaggerated praise - to help Gwen grow in confidence and belief in herself?

Five year old Michael has just made his own bed, but the bedclothes are quite twisted and uneven. When his mother comes in, Michael obviously expects praise as he says:

MICHAEL: 'Look, Mummy, I've made my bed all by myself.'

What insincere (or critical) things do parents sometimes say in a situation like this? How might his mother train Michael to make a bed and help him feel good about himself and his efforts?

JANE (10): Will you help me with this homework, Dad? I just can't do it.

In a situation like this, what do some parents do or say that might not be helpful? How could you encourage Jane - not just taking over and doing everything for her?

Billy is three years old and has just arrived home from the supermarket with his mother. He lifts the carton of eggs, opens it and begins to put the eggs into the hollows in the fridge, saying:

BILLY: 'I'm going to put the eggs into the fridge, Mummy.'

In a situation like this, what do some parents do or say that might not be helpful? What might be helpful for Billy and give him a sense of being able to contribute?

TIPS FOR PARENTS

It is worth learning to encourage effectively, for it is probably the most important and powerful skill a parent can use and it affects all the other skills. Encouraging can become a way of life, an outlook that leaves *you* more contented and does enormous good for your children.

It often helps to postpone correction. On-the-spot correction has been compared to waving at flies to make them go away.

There are three important ways of encouraging: 1. Notice the improvement or effect: 'This place looks a lot tidier now.' 2. Notice the effort: 'Thanks for spending so much time at it - I know it wasn't easy.' 3. Make a personal statement, showing the effect on *you*: 'Thanks for taking the baby - it gave me a good break' or 'I like the way you handled that.'

It is not helpful to compare your children to each other or to others. That encourages competition rather than co-operation.

Be on the lookout every day for efforts, improvements or co-operation in your children, and let them know how their contribution helped, etc.

Avoid exaggeration. Tell the child honestly and sincerely what you appreciate. Even a nod of the head or a comment like 'Sounds good'/ 'Okay'/ 'Good point'/ 'Might work' can be more encouraging than going into too much detail.

It can be more encouraging for children to help them see for *themselves* the merits of what they do - rather than to praise them by telling them what *you* judge or think.

What you *do* can be more encouraging than anything you *say*. It is most encouraging to children, for example, to spend time listening to them and enjoying their company - that is a powerful way of saying: 'I like being with you - you are interesting and fun to be with.' Giving responsibility to children can also be tremendously encouraging to them. It tells them: 'I trust you. You are a responsible person.' A look that says 'I care' can be very encouraging - or a gentle touch. And what can be more encouraging than good humour and a smile!

Psychologists tell us: *'Behaviour that is noticed increases; behaviour that is ignored decreases.'* If you notice bad behaviour and ignore good behaviour, you are doing the exact opposite to what your child needs.

CHAPTER 4: LISTENING

Mr. Power has just come home from work. He is in a grumpy, unpleasant mood and has already complained about the noise from the radio. One of the children turned down the volume, but he is not satisfied.

'If you don't turn off that radio this instant,' he says, 'I'll get up and break the bloody thing!'

Recognising feelings.

This incident illustrates a common problem that can have a terrible effect on family life. Not recognising feelings. Our own feelings and the feelings of others.

It is very easy to blame children for our own annoyance and anger. But is that fair? Our feelings come from inside us. They depend on what we believe. For example, if we think children should do exactly what we say, then we can be very *upset* when they act differently. If we think children should *choose* how to act, then we can be quite *proud* to see them make their own decisions. So we can learn to change our feelings by changing the way we look at a situation. We don't need to bury anger alive.

At the same time, it is important to know that many parents sometimes feel murderous rage towards their children. These feelings are quite normal and are not bad - since they are not acted upon. It is very frightening, of course, for young children to be exposed to very strong adult feelings, so a parent needs to find ways of expressing these feelings, away from children, talking them out with a partner, or even thumping the bed in a locked bedroom.

Parents may also feel discouraged and guilty and see themselves as failures when their children cause problems. But they should not blame themselves for their children's inherited characteristics. There are difficulties and problems associated with every child. All children would seem to have their own task in life to perform. Parents have not created these difficulties and they should try not to let guilt influence them in dealing with them.

Non-listening - and its effects.

So much for parents' feelings. What about children's? If feelings are so important, how can parents learn to recognise what is going on inside their children and give them some sense of being understood? For that sense of being understood can free children from deep-seated feelings that are at the root of so much of their misbehaviour. Let's look at how parents normally deal with their children's feelings.

Many parents are sad today that their children, especially their teenagers, will not communicate with them. But how do these parents listen? What do they say when the children tell them about some trouble they got into? Or are the children afraid to talk because their parents have so often lectured or scolded them in similar situations? As a result, parents often miss chances to help children deal with their feelings.

Much of the advice given to children is well-intentioned, of course, but it is often not helpful. Parents can turn their children away by preaching at them, threatening them, lecturing them, criticising them, cross-questioning them, being sarcastic - or even by *consoling* them!

For consoling, too, can be a form of non-listening. When children are upset, they need to express their feelings. But some parents tell them: 'Don't cry' or 'Don't be upset' or 'You'll feel okay tomorrow' or 'Don't worry, I'll buy you another one.' They mean well, but they are not giving the children what they *most* need in these cases, a sense of being listened to and understood.

Children who are distressed need to express their hurt. They often do this in screams, tears, shaking, laughing, or shouting. They may need to be held to prevent them from hurting others or doing damage, but it is important for parents to encourage that release rather than attempt to smother it by distracting the child or insisting that little boys should not cry. At a time like this, children need a parent's full attention - touching or hugging if necessary - so that they can express their upset feelings and be free to move on. This kind of understanding and attention is a form of listening that communicates respect, love and acceptance, and it frees a child to change, to love, to grow as a person.

How to listen effectively.
That kind of listening does not come naturally, but it is a skill that can be learnt with practice. Here are some ways to become a better listener:

Listen not only with your ears but with your whole body - with your face, your voice, the way you sit forward... It is best to stop working or reading or looking at television and to *look* at the child - but not to stare! The right *words* are not enough if your child senses a lack of openness or understanding in your face or in your tone of voice. So it is important to concentrate on the child and on making the effort to understand. A smile or a frown can make all the difference. And touching *may* also be helpful at times, if you are sensitive to that.

People sometimes think that good listening depends on asking the right questions, but have you ever noticed how threatening, even frightening, questions can be? Some recent research points to the fact that questions often contain a good deal of aggression. Questions, then, may not be helpful if you want to communicate more with your children. Try instead to change the question to 'I don't know....' or 'I wonder...' In this way you are beginning by exposing your ignorance. 'I don't know what you're going to do with that saw' is a better start than: 'What are you going to do with that saw?' If you must ask a question 'What' may be less threatening than 'Why' - and it is important to allow a good pause to give the child time to put the question together and come up with an answer.

Good listening sometimes means remaining silent. Sometimes it can be an understanding grunt or 'yes' or 'I see.' Sometimes it may mean asking a gentle question or telling a similar story from your own experience. At other times, a question or story may be most unsuitable - if it stops the flow or seems to leave the speaker less open. That is the acid test - is your listening helping the speaker to talk, to trust, to be more open, to clarify, to make his or her own decisions, to feel understood. The secret of good listening is to listen beyond the words, beyond the story, beyond the details, to discover the *feelings,* the *person*. And it often helps to check out in your own words that you are hearing those feelings correctly. This is called *active* listening.

Active listening.

Active listening is a term used by Dr Thomas Gordon in his book 'Parent Effectiveness Training.' It means grasping what your child is *really* saying, *really* feeling - then playing that feeling back in your own words with understanding and with caring. This is often called 'empathy.' With this skill, you try to feel what your child is feeling; and you check that you understand by playing back what you hear. Here is an example.

Joe: I'm finished with Paul! He's mean... and stupid!

Mother: You sound very annoyed with him...

Joe: I hate him!

Mother: It's as strong as that. You're very mad with him!

Joe: Yeah. I loaned him my bike and he left it in the mud.

Mother: Oh! And you were so pleased with your new bike!

Joe: Yeah. I'm going to have to clean it all up now...

This approach may seem artificial and strange at first, but it is not something to be used all the time. It is particularly suitable when someone has strong feelings. Upset or excited children *need* to express their feelings, and they will not find active listening the slightest bit strange when used properly. They can feel understood, they can begin to see more clearly what is happening and they can think their way better through a problem. This kind of listening also opens up communication between parent and child. It creates an atmosphere of understanding in a family. It encourages a child to trust, to say more, to talk about difficult areas like feelings, friends, sex, drugs, etc. And it has great power to heal.

We'll look at another example. Ruth has just been told that she may not go to a mid-week disco because of school work.

Ruth: You're always saying no! You hate me, don't you!

Father: You think I'm not being fair, and your angry with me.

Ruth: Fair! You're a dictator. Always laying down the law.

Father: You see me just tying you down with rules?

Ruth: Yeah!

Father: So you're fed up with the rules...

Ruth: Yeah. I'm treated like a little four year old around here - only a four year old would have more freedom!

Father: You feel I don't trust you.

Ruth: Exactly! You *don't* trust me.

Father: I see... Sounds like you're very mad with me about that...

Notice that Ruth's feelings are very strong. This kind of mirror-listening is only to be used when feelings *are* strong - otherwise it would come across as artificial and unreal. Notice too that the father was careful not to use the exact same words as his daughter and that he kept trying to play back the *feelings* as well. It may seem that he didn't get very far, but he kept calm and allowed Ruth the freedom to express her anger. He may not see immediate results, but Ruth will now be more capable of coming to terms with her problem.

Contrast that with what often happens in this kind of situation and you can see why communication can break down so easily in families, especially between parents and teenagers.

Not just a problem-solving skill

The active listening approach can also be a good one when a child asks certain questions. If parents suspect that there may be more behind the question they can check that out by playing back what they think the child's curiosities or fears are. When Malcolm asks: 'Why is grass green?' Mother can reply: 'That's a silly question,' or 'because it's always green!' or she may check out: 'You're wondering if grass can sometimes change colour?' That can become an opportunity to show a young child how grass turns yellow and white when a plank or stone is left on it and how the older grass dies and turns brown in winter or during a dry spell. Good listening opens up many possibilities, not only for solving problems, but for improving the whole parent-child relationship.

Active listening, then is much more than a mere technique or skill. It is one of the most effective ways of expressing love, because it demands genuine concern and understanding. A child notices when there is a lack of understanding or caring.

How to begin.
Parents trying to improve their listening pay attention to what their children say and then guess at what *feelings* lie behind that. Here are some common words used to express feelings. Angry, annoyed, anxious, afraid, appreciated, bored, cheated, comfortable, confident, delighted, disappointed, depressed, disgusted, embarrassed, excited, fed-up, furious, glad, great, happy, guilty, hopeless, hurt, left out, mad, miserable, over the moon, proud, put down, relaxed, relieved, sad, satisfied, shy, silly, stupid, thankful, upset, useless, willing, worried.

Here are some examples of these feelings which children do not express (in brackets and italics beside what they say):

You don't have to tell me what to do! *(I feel humiliated, very small, unimportant..)* I wish I didn't live here! *(I feel angry, hurt.)* I hate school! *(I feel bored, useless, miserable.)* You call that love-making? - it sounds disgusting! *(I'm embarrassed, uncomfortable with my own body.)* I can't sleep. *(I feel tense, upset, confused.)*

When a child's feelings seem clear, the parent can then play that feeling back: 'You feel...' 'You're very...' 'You seem to be...' 'Sounds as if you're...' The aim is to allow the child to open up, to say more. So try not to play back the feeling much stronger or much weaker than it is. Otherwise, the child may close up again.

It is probably worth repeating that active listening is artificial and unhelpful if overdone. When your daughter complains that her brother has got a bigger helping of dinner, it may be better to say something humorous: 'Yes, dear, we like him more than we like you!' Used at the appropriate time, however, active listening is one of the most powerful skills a parent can have.

Finally, it will take time to learn and be at ease with active listening. Like any new skill, it may feel awkward at first, but with practice and patience it soon becomes quite natural.

GETTING IN TOUCH

For each of the children's comments below decide what parents usually say that is not helpful. Then ask yourself what the child might really be thinking and feeling.
'I don't want to go to school tomorrow'
'You don't care about me'
'Our teacher is mean!'

 # PLANS FOR NEXT WEEK

To which child will you give a good experience of being listened to and understood this week? What would be a *natural* time for that? (Bedtime?... When they're upset?... Or over a special supper?...) How will you begin? What might help your child to trust you and say more? You may like to write down what you plan.

Plans..._____

TABLE 4: LISTENING

Consider the following examples of helpful and unhelpful responses to what children say. The examples given in the 'Helpful listening' column show the **attitude** *of the parents rather than the actual words they might use, of course - the words will vary according to the situation.*

Child says:	Unhelpful approach	Helpful listening
1. You don't have to tell me what to do.	Oh, yes I do - I'm your father and you'll do what you're told.	It makes you angry when I seem to be ordering you around...
2. I hate Margaret. I'm not going to play anymore!	You mustn't hate people, dear. I'm sure she didn't mean it!	Mm. I see... So you're upset with Margaret...
3. I'm just no good at maths.	Well, you'll just have to keep trying.	You sound a bit hopeless about maths... You're finding it very difficult.
4. Why can't I go too! She's only a year older than me.	That's enough. We're not going to talk any more about it!	You're feeling a bit cheated - it doesn't seem fair to you.
5. Our team won, Mum!	That's good! Now go and wash you hands.	Oh! You' must be delighted!
6. The arm of my new doll is smashed. (*child crying*).	Don't worry, love, I'll buy you a new one.	(Hug) And you were so pleased with your new doll. That is *so* upsetting!

CASE STUDIES

(Alternative to listening to the audio tapes)

Read the following conversations (it may be better if two or three people read them aloud). Then, in groups of three, discuss the questions at the end of each situation.

LUCY (9): I've nothing to do! I called for Sheila but she's gone off on her holidays.
FATHER: Oh well, you can always get someone else to play with you.
What feelings might Lucy have had when she arrived home? If you were Lucy, what effect might your father's remark have had on you? How could he use active listening to show understanding instead?

Twelve year old Pat is talking to his mother:
PAT: I hate my teacher. He's the meanest man I've ever met. I wish he was dead!
MOTHER: That's no way to talk about anyone! You must have been doing something wrong if he's down on you.
How do you think Pat may have been feeling about himself and his school and his teacher? If you were Pat, what effect might your mother's remark have had on you? How could she use active listening and help him express some of his feelings?

DAVID (5, close to tears): Richard and Joe sent me away. They said I'm too small to play with them.
MOTHER: Don't worry, David. You're better off without friends like that!
If you were David, how would you feel if your friends had treated you in this way? What effect might his mother's remark have had on him? What might have helped instead? A hug? A listening ear? How might she use active listening?

Ten year old Tom has been at his homework for over half an hour.
TOM: This homework is too difficult for me. I give up.
MOTHER: Well, you can't afford to give up. You just haven't stuck at it long enough. You need to keep trying.
How do you think Tom feels about his homework? If you were Tom, what effect might your mother's remark have had on you? How can she use active listening and help him express some of his feelings?

ANNA (17): Dad, guess what! Mike has asked me to go to the disco!
FATHER: Well you just make sure you're in before one o'clock!
How do you think Anna feels about her date? What effect might her father's remark have on her? How can he use active listening instead?

TIPS FOR PARENTS

There are some special times when it helps to set everything aside and concentrate on listening to children: when they come home from school (they may have little to say, but just try to be present to them); bedtime; and when they appear to have strong feelings (upset, excited, depressed).

Parents can shut off listening by nagging, scolding, bossing, advising, cross-questioning, not paying attention, being sarcastic, and by consoling. All of these can cause breakdown in communication between parents and their children. See how you can lessen them.

When a child is upset about his broken toy, or crying because her big brother pulled her hair, or depressed about having no friends, what that child needs most is *listening*, a sense of being *understood*. Unfortunately, parents often think it is their duty to come up with solutions. Whereas listening and understanding is actually the *beginning*

of the solution and sometimes the *only* solution that is needed

When you're listening to children, it usually helps to stoop down to their level. That can make it easier for them to talk.

One of the best ways of listening to an upset child can be a hug that allows the child to express the upset feelings in tears.

You can encourage your child to say more with a comment like: 'Yes' or 'I see' or by playing back feelings: 'You felt bad about that.' That is usually more helpful than a direct question.

If you must ask a question, try to be sensitive and gentle in the way you put it. 'I don't know...' or 'I wonder...' can be a good way to start.

For active listening:
1. Listen for feelings.
2. Try to put a name on the feeling.
3. Check out with your child if you are right.
4. Let the child clarify or correct you if you've got the feeling wrong.

It is usually not helpful to correct on the spot, particularly when you are angry and upset. Correction or advice is usually more effective later, at a calm time. And in the middle of a crisis, it is especially unhelpful to preach or advise or say, 'I told you so!'

CHAPTER 5 - COMMUNICATING ABOUT PROBLEMS

Vincent, thirteen, made a snack for himself and sat watching television without clearing anything away. When his mother saw the mess, she felt like screaming at him to clear it up. She wanted to tell him she was not his maid - and to remind him of how often she had told him to clear up after himself. Instead, she stayed calm, called him, and said, 'Vincent, I've spent a long time cleaning the kitchen, and when you leave it like this I feel very discouraged.' Vincent said he was sorry and cleaned it up right away. The mother's approach had worked because she had used what Dr Thomas Gordon calls an 'I-message.' With an I-message parents tell their children as honestly and as calmly as possible how they feel. Let's look at another example.

Father and mother were having a sleep-in on Saturday morning. At seven thirty, Jacqueline, five, came into her parents' room, woke up her father, crawled on top of him and wanted to 'play.' Father was in no mood for play. He felt impatient and wanted to say to her as crossly as possible, 'What do you mean by wakening me up!

Couldn't you see I was asleep! Now get out of this room and stop being a little nuisance.' Instead, he gave Jacqueline an I-message, 'Jackie, I'm feeling very sleepy and tired - much too sleepy to play with you. It's very early, but if you want to play, you can play with toys in your room.' Jacqueline went back to her room. She may not have been very satisfied, but at least she hadn't suffered as a result of an explosion from her father. Telling her his feelings had helped.

In the last chapter, we saw how active listening can help when a child has a problem. In the same way, an I-message can help when the *parent* has a problem.

Who owns the problem?

So it is important to be clear first about who *owns* a problem - the parent, or the child, or both? When Vincent left the kitchen in a mess, Vincent himself may have been quite happy. His mother was not happy about it, so she owned the problem - the untidy kitchen was upsetting to her and was interfering with her rights. On the other hand, if Vincent is upset because he has no friends, his mother can 'help' him much more effectively when she first of all recognises that it is *Vincent* who owns this problem. This is an important distinction, for parents need to take two different approaches depending on who owns a problem. Let's look then at a way of helping children deal with problems that *they* own.

When the child owns the problem

How do parents usually approach their children's problems? Sometimes they criticise the child, nagging, lecturing and scolding, and pointing out mistakes. Other parents show more understanding - they take the child aside and offer advice. Often enough, that is not helpful. Firstly, it may not be the right advice; secondly, children can have a built-in resistance to their parents' advice; thirdly (and most important), it can run contrary to the whole notion of responsible parenthood. Responsible parents *need* to give advice at times, but, whenever possible, it is best to work with children in helping them find their *own* solutions. The following four stages have been found useful in doing this:

1. **Start with active listening.** This helps your child to understand the situations more clearly. 'You're very worried about your exams...'

2. **Begin together to think up possible solutions.** (This is often called brainstorming.) 'What do you think you might be able to do about this?' Try to get a number of different ideas - and these ideas can be written down. It may help to ask: 'What would you like to see happening?' Establish your own rights too by then telling your child what *you* would like to see happening?'

3. **Help your child to choose one idea.** Look together at the advantages, disadvantages and results of each idea until one emerges which seems satisfactory. It may help to write down what you decide. 'Which of these ideas seems best to you?' 'When will you do this?' 'For how long?'...

4. **Fix a time for reviewing how the plan is working.** 'When will we get together again to see how things are going?'

These four stages apply if the *child* owns the problem. What happens, however, when it is the *parent* who owns the problem?

When you own the problem

What usually happens when parents have problems with children? Very often, they correct their children with 'you-messages.' 'You've left the door open!' 'You didn't clean the mud off your shoes!' 'You've taken too much milk.' Even if the parent does not add something more insulting, the child can easily feel humiliated and attacked by the remark - if not by the tone of voice as well. That is not a respectful approach, nor an effective one. Parents need to be able to confront their children without condemning them and to assert themselves in such a way that there are no winners or losers.

I-messages are much more effective and helpful. When parents give I-messages, they say honestly and gently how they feel about the result of their children's behaviour. An I message does not blame. For example, 'When you take a lot of milk, I'm concerned that there won't be enough to go around'; 'When we agree together on a bedtime and then you stay up late, I feel very uneasy, because I don't know where we stand with each other.' 'When you leave your things scattered over the dining-room floor, I feel ashamed to take people in.'

I-messages will not solve all your problems. They will solve *some* problems, but correction - and sometimes action - will often be called for too. The point is that an I-message (not moaning, not blaming, not critical) shows respect for a child and can be the *beginning* of a solution. Even a simple statement of feelings like: 'I'm just in rotten form today' is so much more helpful than acting out feelings, blaming and making a child feel guilty and bad.

Giving I-messages.

Have you noticed in the examples that the concentration is not usually on the child's *behaviour* but on its *results*. When you want to give an I-message, then, it is recommended that you express it something like this, 'When... I feel... because...' For example, 'When you put your feet up on the couch, it worries me because it's quite new and I would hate it to get soiled or damaged.'

Parents sometimes claim that I-messages do not work for them. Often enough, this is because these parents begin with 'I feel' and then give a strong you-message, 'I feel angry when you can't behave yourself and you go around bullying your little brother like that!' So try to stick to genuine *feelings* and to avoid blaming, even with your tone of voice. I-messages should not be over-used. For this reason it is best to avoid strong negative feelings like anger. Anger is usually a surface feeling when someone is really feeling disappointed, embarrassed, or hurt, so it is more helpful to say, 'I feel so *embarrassed* when my friends come in and you don't speak to them, because I would like them to feel welcome in our home.'

It helps to give your children I-messages about your positive feelings as well, 'I'm delighted with the job you did in the backyard. It's so much nicer to go out there when it's tidy.' And one of the most powerful of all I-messages is the simple, 'I'm sorry. Will you forgive me?' Asking forgiveness of children and reconciling with them are great for parenting.

The two approaches.
Let's sum up then. This chapter deals with situations where you or your children have problems - about misbehaviour, disrespect, bedtimes, pocket money, chores, watching TV, unsuitable friends, blaring music, etc., etc. There are two different approaches, depending on who owns the problem. So it helps to start by asking yourself, 'Who owns this problem - me or my child?'

If *you* own the problem, ask, 'What are the results of this behaviour, and how do I honestly feel about them?' Then give an I-message, saying how you feel about these results. If your child owns the problem, it usually helps to use active listening. For more serious problems it may be best to withdraw from the conflict and suggest a time for talking the problem out together. The four steps for solving problems can then be followed.

Talking out a problem, as we have seen, is not always enough. Action is often needed as well. In the next chapter, we will look at suitable action that can be taken, but it is always good to straighten out the lines of communication first.

GETTING IN TOUCH

See if you can decide who owns each of the following problems - the parent or the child. *(To decide who owns a problem, it usually helps to ask, 'Who is unhappy or upset in this situation?' Occasionally, of course, parents allow* **themselves** *to get upset when it is the* **child** *who owns the problem, but this guideline should work for you most of the time.)*

1. Child dilly-dallies over dressing and breakfast - then doesn't do chore.
2. In spite of being called, your twelve year old daughter has slept in and is now late for school.
3. Your two year old child begins to climb a ladder.
4. Your child is disrespectful to you in front of neighbours.
5. Your four year old and six year old are constantly squabbling and fighting.
6. Your son is bullying a neighbour's child.
7. Homework is untidy or not being done at all.
8. Bedtimes are being ignored.
9. Your teenager is drifting with the crowd and not working at school.

PLANS FOR NEXT WEEK

1. Try giving one clear, well-thought-out I-message to someone each day for the next week - you'll only get better by practising.

2. Set aside time to go through the stages of problem-solving with a child this week. With which child? What would be a good problem to start with? When will you do this? You may like to write down what you plan.

Plans..._____

_____

TABLE 5: COMMUNICATING ABOUT PROBLEMS

This Table shows the two different approaches parents can take, depending on who owns a problem. Sometimes a problem belongs to both parent and child, but it is usually obvious who most owns it. Could you add to this Table from your own experience of problem situations with children?

Problem	Who owns it	Caution	Active Listening	I-Message
1. Child regularly leaves door open.	Parent	Try not to blame - focus on *results* of door being left open.		'When the door is left open, I feel quite cold in this draught.'
2. Child crying because older brother called her names.	Child	Try not to interfere in children's squabbles except in cases of danger.	(Hug) 'You're terribly upset...'	
3. Five year old is trying to cut bread with sharp knife.	Parent	Try not to panic. Watch tone of voice - alarm creates alarm and nervousness.		(Calmly) 'When you use the sharp knife, I feel nervous in case you cut yourself.'
4. Child has been ignored by a friend.	Child	It doesn't help to pretend if doesn't matter - nor to 'solve' the child's problem.	'You're feeling angry and hurt...'	
5. Child leaves your tools out in the rain.	Parent	Try not to scold or criticise.		'I feel annoyed when the tools are left outside - I'm afraid they may get rusty or lost or even stolen.'
6. Child hates school.	Child	Be slow to advise - it probably won't help.	'You're feeling useless and lost at school...'	

CASE STUDIES

(Alternative to listening to the audio tapes)

Form groups of three and discuss the situations below. In each case, decide who owns the problem - the parent or the child. If the child owns the problem, see how you might use active listening and show understanding without taking over the problem (though it's not appropriate to use active listening every time a child has a problem)! If the parent owns the problem, see if you can give a suitable I-message to communicate how you feel (though that can also be overdone)

- You're trying to have a chat with a neighbour who seldom calls and who is quite lonely, but your six year old daughter keeps interrupting you.
- Eleven year old Mark was going down town on his bicycle. A minute later, he comes back to the house looking fed-up. 'Aw, dad,' he says, 'Guess what! My front wheel's punctured! What am I going to do?'
- Mother is about to make the dinner when she finds that her four year old has left toys scattered all over the kitchen floor.
- Your sixteen year old daughter, Elizabeth, comes in, looking pale. She announces that she has just failed an important exam.

Here is a shortened version of what can happen with skilled use of the four stages of problem solving. Can you pick out each of the four stages as the mother uses them? (It may help to look at the four stages in chapter five.)

Jeremy: (Slams door.) There's far too much work in this house. Tidy your room! Clear the table! Sweep the floor! Wash the dishes!... I hate living here!

Mother: Seems like a lot of work, Jeremy. Makes you fed up...

Jeremy: Yeah. Other boys don't have to do anything at home!

Mother: So that leaves you feeling a bit cheated - like it's a real burden for you.

Jeremy: Yeah, that's right. But it never stops.

Mother: So what do you think you could do about it?

Jeremy: There's nothing *I* can do about it. *I* don't make the decisions around here.

Mother: Well, if you could decide, what would be a fair thing to do.

Jeremy: (uncooperatively) Well, you're the grown-ups. *You* should do the work.

Mother: That's one possibility. Anything else that might be fair.

Jeremy: Pay someone to come in and do the work.

Mother: That's two suggestions. Any more?

Jeremy: You could at least share out jobs so one person doesn't end up doing so much.

Mother: Mm. That's three things we might do. Dad and I do the jobs. Pay someone else to do them. Or share them out in the family. Which idea do you think is best?

Jeremy (softening): Well, the first two ideas are the easiest... But it really wouldn't be fair to you and Dad. (pause) *Could* we pay someone?

Mother: We couldn't afford that... So where does that leave us?

Jeremy: Share out the jobs, I suppose.

Mother: Are you willing to do your share?

Jeremy: As long as my job isn't going to take too long. What would I have to do?

Mother: What would you prefer to do?

Jeremy: Mm... I'll set the table and clear it.

Mother: Right. But I don't want to be running around after you reminding you. Are you sure you're prepared to do this?

Jeremy: Look, would I say it if I wasn't prepared to do it!

Mother: Okay. Let's try it for a week and we'll see then how it works. Is that all right with you?

Jeremy: Mm. Okay.

TIPS FOR PARENTS

Decide who owns the problem, i.e. who is most unhappy or upset? If *you* own the problem, try giving an I-message. If your *child* owns the problem, try active listening.

For bigger or thorny problems, try brainstorming as well - thinking up, and perhaps writing down, possible solutions. It's surprising how many possibilities two people can come up with when they put their minds to it.

When brainstorming, it is best not to tell your children the snags you see in their suggestions. Try instead to help them with gentle questions to see for themselves what the snags and advantages are.

Help children to *choose* solutions to their problems. Solutions imposed by parents may not encourage a child to be responsible.

Solving problems can be a waste of time if you don't also make time to look back and see how the solution is working out in practice.

When *you* own a problem, an I-message helps, because it treats the child with respect. It is usually best to focus on the *results* of the child's behaviour.

When giving I-messages, it may be better not to use strong negative feelings like anger. Tell your child about the embarrassment, disappointment or hurt *beneath* your anger. Feelings about *yourself* are often the best ones to share -helpless, alone, a sense of failure as a parent.

If you children are still too young to use the different stages of problem-solving, you may like to practise solving problems with a partner. Many couples find these four stages useful in dealing constructively with conflict in their own lives.

CHAPTER 6: DISCIPLINING CHILDREN

Patrick, fourteen, was sitting with his feet on the couch, reading a magazine. His mother decided to give him an I-message, since this was obviously her problem.

'Patrick, when you put your feet up on the couch, it worries me because it's quite new and I would hate it to get dirty.'

Patrick didn't budge. He grunted and said, 'I like sitting this way. It's more comfortable.' He continued to read.

'Patrick, either sit properly on the couch or sit any way you like on the floor. Which do you want to do?'

He scowled, but he put his feet on the floor and sat back on the couch. His mother had treated him with respect by giving him an I-message, but, when that had not worked, she offered him a choice. She did not scold, nag, threaten, punish or coax - but she had used an effective method of discipline.

Learning from consequences.

For many parents, the normal way to discipline children is to punish them - or to reward them. Neither way seems to be effective in the long term. If we want to have responsible children, they need to learn to take responsibility for their *own* behaviour - rather than to be constantly looking over their shoulders to see if we approve or disapprove. Forcing children to do things our way, moreover, may only encourage them to rebel as soon as they get a chance - genuine love, we are told, 'does not insist on its own way.'

It is generally more effective and responsible to allow children to make their own decisions when possible - and to learn from the consequences of what they choose. If children choose not to eat, they may feel a little hunger until the next meal. If they refuse to wear coats, they may feel cold and will learn from that experience. These are natural consequences of their decisions.

Allowing children to choose.

The secret of good discipline, then, is to allow children to choose, except when there is real danger. When they misbehave, try not to nag, lecture or punish but to offer a choice, 'I can't stand this noise at the table. Either stop the squabbling or go outside.

You decide.' If your two small children continue to squabble, you can take it that they have chosen to leave the table, but again you can offer a choice, 'I see you've chosen to go outside. Do you want to leave the room yourselves or would you prefer me to carry you out?' They usually keep their dignity by choosing to leave the room themselves! If there is no answer, however, you might gently carry both children out of the room, assuring them, 'You're welcome to come back in when you have decided to settle down.' You are still offering them choices and treating them with respect. In a short time, they will have learnt a great deal from the consequences of their choices.

Here is another example. Twelve year old George lies on in the morning and keeps everyone late for school. You decide with the children what time they would like to leave in the car and then announce, 'Okay, from now on, I'll leave at that time. Anyone who is not ready will have to walk to school and accept the consequences of dealing with the teacher. Is that agreed?' Be flexible - allow for a genuine emergency - but in general it is important to be firm in sticking to your side of the agreement.

Using consequences is not a method of punishment.

When parents discipline their children by using consequences, these consequences should flow naturally or logically out of the situation. If Jack breaks a window, it may follow logically that he has to pay towards a new one, but it would not be appropriate to stop his pocket-money because of not keeping his room tidy - in that case, there is no logical connection between money and his behaviour. Instead, you could say, 'I've just vacuumed the house, but there were a lot of things on your floor, so I'll leave the vacuum cleaner here for you to do it.' Jack then has to live with the *real* consequences of keeping his room untidy. Or when Susan has agreed to go to bed at 10 o'clock but breaks her agreement, you might say, 'For the next two days we'll go back to the old arrangement of bedtime at 9.30, Susan. Then we'll try the 10 o'clock agreement

again.' Notice that there isn't any hint of punishment here, and the possibility of a new start is always presented. It generally helps to say something like, 'You can try again tomorrow.' Reminding children of the fresh start avoids humiliating them and it also helps the parent to stay friendly.

There are other ways to avoid using consequences as punishment. Try not to get angry, to remind, to threaten, to warn, or to say something like, 'Maybe this will teach you!' - action is much more effective than talking. It is important to be firm but gentle - even to invite a young child, 'Let's clear up this mess together,' rather than always give a choice. Indeed, it can help to remind yourself that the *purpose* of using consequences is to help children make responsible decisions - not to force them to do your will. So this method of discipline should not be used to bolster up parents' decisions except in the case of very young children. It helps to involve the children in the first place in making the decision (about bedtime, about which chores to do, about whether or not they want to go on an outing, etc.).

Thinking up consequences.

'That is all very well,' some parents protest, 'But most of the time I cannot even *think* of a logical consequence, so I fall back on my old methods of nagging and dictating!' When you cannot think of a consequence, there is a temptation to make a snap decision. One useful tip is to postpone your decision and withdraw from conflict, especially when there is a lot of tension between you and your child. That gives you a chance to think. Another tip is to ask your *children* about the consequences of their own actions or misbehaviour. When Jim loses your saw, you don't necessarily have to think of a consequence yourself. You could ask, 'How are you going to get me a new saw, Jim?' When children have just had a row, you might ask, 'I wonder what other things you could have done to each other instead of hitting and using violence when you were so angry?' In this way, their options are also being increased and widened.

It may also help to bear in mind that a choice doesn't always sound like a choice, for example when you use what we might call the 'as soon as' method - 'Yes, you can go out to play as soon as the dishes are washed and dried,' 'Yes, you may watch TV as soon as you've tidied your bedroom.' 'Yes, you can have the dessert as soon as you've eaten your dinner,' 'I'm putting the bike away now, but you can use it again as soon as you come to an agreement about it that will stop the squabbling.' In these cases, the child is really being given a choice. You're not insisting on the dinner being eaten; you are allowing the child to choose and to live with the consequences of not eating it. At the same time, you are reminding the child about a chore that has previously been agreed, but your statement is a positive one. Isn't it better to say 'You can read your comic as soon as you've vacuumed the floor' than to say 'No, you can't read your comic. You haven't vacuumed the floor!' Positive communication is the key to this entire programme as well as to good long-term discipline.

Stay firm.
Applying consequences requires a certain firmness and strength (but not harshness) from parents. Neighbours and friends, even teachers, sometimes expect you to be a 'good' parent rather than a responsible one; they may criticise you for not making sure that your children arrive at school on time (though it can help to have a word with the teacher about what you are doing). You may also feel guilty if your children dilly-dally and don't take responsibility for making lunch in time, then have to rush off to school without their lunches. But it is important to stay firm. These are excellent learning experiences for children. You can see them become responsible as a result. Adults learn all the time from consequences - if they go to the shop without money, or if they forget to buy something in the super-market.

It may be important to bear in mind that using consequences is only *one* method of discipline. The truth is that *all* the skills of this course are closely linked to discipline. But *some* form of discipline is essential. 'Spoilt' children, who get every-thing they ask for, and are constantly given their own way, can become their own worst enemies. Lack of limits can leave them feeling insecure and unsure of boundaries. Worst of all, not having limits can actually prevent them from testing out and dis-covering who they are - which Eric Erikson has highlighted as their most important task in life! Limits are that important.

Here, then, are some more examples of how parents can foster good discipline by using consequences.

Examples of consequences.
Mother is buying shoes for her two year old, Billy. He has taken a fancy to sandals instead. She tells him that they are not suitable, so he throws a tantrum. This is a power-struggle and he is testing his strength against hers, sensing how embarr-assing his misbehaviour in public can be. However, she does not give in. She leaves the shoe shop. It is not the end of the world if he has to do without new shoes for a few days. She does not scold. She explains that they can go back to the shoe shop when he is prepared to behave. Even a two year old understands consequences very quickly.

Nancy is five years old. She keeps finding excuses to get out of bed after being settled each evening. So her father makes sure she has been to the toilet, etc., then announces, 'If you get up again, I'll turn off the night-light in the hallway to help you sleep. You decide.' If she gets up again, father turns off the light, saying, 'I'm turning off the light, but we'll try again tomorrow.' She may cry to see if father will change his mind. Father does not allow himself to be manipulated by her crying. He allows her to learn from the consequences of her own behaviour. (But he listens to what Nancy has to say through her tears - that will sometimes reveal an underlying worry.)

Eight year old Martin is invited to a birthday party and his parents say he can go if he has done his chores. When the time comes, he has not done his chores but begs to be allowed to go. His parents refuse gently but firmly. When he continues to plead, they leave the room.

Deirdre, ten, does not want to go to school - she says she is not feeling well (though she may be foxing). Her father is sympathetic but insists that if she stays home from school she must spend the day in bed, since she is ill. Deirdre then makes her own choice.

Eleven year old Robert and thirteen year old Edward are fighting in the car. Their mother stops the car and explains, 'I find it impossible to drive while this fighting is going on. I want you to settle down or else to leave the car and walk home. Which do you want to do?' This is not a threat. She accepts their decision, either way. It is surprising how quickly children get the message.

Fifteen year old Becky comes home later than the time agreed with her mother.

Her mother says, 'Becky, you and I agreed that you'd be home by 11.00 p.m. Since you haven't kept your side of the agreement, I want you to be home by 10.30 for the next week. After a week, we'll try the 11.00 o'clock agreement again.' If Becky's time-keeping does not improve after a week, the length of time before she can try again may have to be extended.

All these are examples of *possible* lines of action in line with consequences. There are many other possibilities of course. What they all have in common is *action* with very little talking. Try to talk as little as possible when operating consequences. Applying consequences in these ways is an effective, non-violent method of dealing with the constant discipline problems which affect every family. Properly understood, it is also a method that is deeply respectful to children.

GETTING IN TOUCH

What do parents normally do or say when a child:
1. Throws a tantrum at home?
2. Throws a tantrum in public?
3. Won't get up in the morning?
4. Watches TV instead of doing homework?
5. Stays out an hour later than permitted?
6. Refuses to co-operate with the family, do chores etc.?
7. Dresses in what seems to be an outlandish or careless way?
8. Teases or bullies a little sister?
9. Is squabbling with another child?
10. Keeps her room very untidy?

PLANS FOR NEXT WEEK

Think of one ongoing discipline problem in your home. How could you begin to deal with it, applying consequences? What would be a good time for talking it out with your child(ren)? How could you present it as a choice rather than as a punishment or an ultimatum? You may like to write down what you plan.

Plans..._____

TABLE 6: APPLYING CONSEQUENCES

This table shows ways of allowing children to learn from the consequences of their choices. Can you see how these ideas might apply in your own family?

Problem	Usual Method of Discipline	Using Consequences	Effect
1. Child not getting up when called.	Shout, nag keep reminding, threaten, coax, force.	Call only once (or give older child alarm clock and allow to be late for school or do without breakfast, if necessary). During school holidays, decide together on breakfast time - those who miss breakfast wait for lunch.	Child will begin to take responsibility for self in the mornings.
2. Child continually forgets things.	Remind, nag, scold, search, rescue.	Let child experience consequences of forgetting lunch, school books, etc. For matters that affect parent, work out an agreed consequence in advance - and apply it.	Child very quickly takes responsibility for remembering.
3. Hair and clothes styles not suitable.	Parent buys child's clothes, decides length of hair, etc.	Allow child greater say in choosing hair style and selecting clothes within reasonable limits. Allow child to get wet or cold (within reason) rather than *insist* on appropriate clothes. For going out *together* insist on your rights - that child be suitably dressed - or leave child behind (if necessary with baby-sitter).	Child learns to choose and make decisions about style and about appropriate clothes.
4. Child doesn't brush teeth.	Remind, scold, shame, force.	Offer choice between brushing teeth and giving up sweet things.	Child brushes teeth - and sees link with dental decay.
5. Chores being ignored.	Remind, nag, shout, pay... Or parent does chore for child.	Agree on family chores together. Establish clearly the consequences for not doing chores, e.g. meal is delayed if dishes are not washed or table not set. Most effective when *all* children suffer together.	Children learn to contribute to smooth running of the home.
6. Bedtimes being ignored.	Remind, nag, have a row, force, punish.	Agree together on a bedtime. If ignored, go back for two days to the earlier bedtime, then try again. For younger children, offer choice - to go to bed or be carried to bed. Repeat as often as child gets up.	Child begins to take responsibility for *own* bedtime.
7. Home-work not being done.	Scold, warn, lecture, or do homework with child.	Take an interest in the homework and possibly help child with it. Ask questions about it and give *necessary* assistance. But let child face consequences from the *teacher* for poor or no homework.	Child takes responsibility for homework, *and* develops relation-ship with parent.
8. Baby eats sand.	Protect, scold, rescue, shout, remind, or frighten.	Calmly remove from sandpit to playpen for short time. If behaviour is repeated, leave child in playpen for longer time. Remain calm.	Child learns to play harmlessly without undue attention.

CASE STUDIES

(Alternative to listening to the audio tapes)

Here are a number of situations which cause problems for parents. Form threes and see if you can decide
1. how parents usually deal with these situations.
2. how you might be able to apply consequences while remaining friendly.

Twelve year old Bob has a habit of forgetting to take things to school with him - sometimes his lunch, sometimes his schoolbag, sometimes his coat. His mother has to put herself to a lot of trouble to get these to him. Each time, she lectures and scolds, and every morning she reminds him to check that he has everything with him. Bob still forgets things and admits that he just seems to be forgetful.

There's a lot of ongoing bickering and squabbling between eight year old Pauline and eleven year old Barry. They tease and taunt and nip and hit each other. There's constant screaming and shouting and running to mother and father with complaints.

Mrs Grant is constantly picking clothes off the floor of the bedrooms and the bathroom - where her children (aged fourteen to nine) have dropped them. She's constantly nagging and scolding about this situation, but this has little effect.

Aileen is three. She shows very little interest in her food except for playing with it. Indeed, she seems to have discovered that she gets lots of attention from her parents in their efforts to coax her to eat and in the praise they lavish on her every time she takes a spoonful. The entire mealtime has even become centred around her eating.

Eighteen year old Alice likes to listen to music when she comes home in the evening. She plays it very loudly on the family stereo in the living-room. The music is too loud for her father and mother.

TIPS FOR PARENTS

There are many ways to discipline children. Much depends on what works with a particular child, what the circumstances are, etc. Sometimes talking things out helps, sometimes encouraging, sometimes taking time for training and giving responsibility. But applying consequences can be an effective way. In applying consequences: 1. Try offering children a choice - this shows respect for them. 2. Act; don't scold. 3. Stay friendly. Remind the child 'You can try again tomorrow.'

If you want to stop *ordering* your child and begin offering choices, try saying 'If...' instead of 'Don't...' Instead of 'Don't cut the bread on the tablecloth,' try, 'If you want to cut the bread, you can use the breadboard.'

Be flexible and sensitive in using consequences - they are for constantly recurring problems rather than for emergencies.

Using consequences is not a method of punishment but an attempt to get children to learn from the choices they make and to become more *responsible*. If they are *not* becoming more responsible or learning to discipline themselves, you may need to take another look at your approach.

Do your best to stay firm in keeping to your side of the agreement. Too many parents make idle threats that they do not intend to carry out. If you agree to have your evening meal at 6.00 p.m. and your son doesn't arrive until 6.30 p.m., it may be good to allow him face the consequences - at least to let him rustle up something for himself - rather than to start preparing an extra meal for him.

When a problem arises, it can sometimes be helpful to start with a good brain-storming session - 'What do any of you think we can do about this?...' That gives the children a sense of being involved in solving the problem themselves.

Strike a balance. Remember the other skills of a responsible parent too. You will not get very far if you attempt to discipline children without using the two more important skills of encouragement and listening.

In disciplining children, it helps to remember the power of your own example in disciplining *yourself.* Just as shouting, interrupting, hitting, cursing, and criticising teaches children to shout, interrupt, hit, curse and criticise, in the same way your gentleness, firmness, honesty, listening, asking forgiveness and encouraging teaches them to be gentle, to be firm, to be honest, to listen, to ask forgiveness and to encourage in turn.

Children desperately need limits, even to kick against. When they fight limits, throw tantrums, or shout 'I hate you,' don't panic or back down; it's important to allow them to express their feelings - even to hold them gently as they kick and scream, and to give them good attention until their tears are spent. Notice how healing that can be for a troubled child.

CHAPTER 7: TALKING THINGS OUT TOGETHER

The Spences (mother, father and three children, aged six to fourteen) had a problem. They often wanted to watch different television programmes at the same time - which led to constant bickering. The parents were also unhappy about the amount of time their children spent watching television - and about some of the programmes they were watching.

As a result of the parenting programme Mr & Mrs Spence decided to sit down with their children and talk things out together. In that way all the family had an opportunity to state how they saw the problem, and how it affected them and what they would like to see happening. After forty minutes, they had gone right through the four stages of problem-solving. Trying to suit everyone and reach agreement was difficult - each one had to compromise and settle for something less than they wanted - but finally they reached agreement on a number of issues.

1. No plays or films after 9.30 p.m. unless a parent is present.

2. No television without planning, but each child can plan to watch 5 hours a week.

3. News, documentaries and educational programmes can be watched at any time in addition to the five hours of television.

As it happens, these arrangements worked reasonably well in practice. But that is not the point - what suits one family can often prove impossible, even depressing, to another family. The point is that the Spences were able to talk out a very difficult area that had been causing a lot of tension and conflict - and they managed to reach agreement, with each one having a real sense of being involved in the solution. They were very brave to tackle such a major area of family life. In general, it is better for a family to start by planning something enjoyable together, like an outing or a holiday - or to begin by dealing with minor problems.

The aim of this course is to build genuine respect between family members. Our aim is to help all the members of a family to co-operate in *making* decisions and to live with the results of what they decide. In the experience of many families, one of the most effective ways to encourage this to happen is to have a regular, perhaps weekly time when each family member can have a chance to talk.

What is a 'family meeting'?

Parents sometimes dislike the idea of a family meeting when they hear of it. 'Why can't we just talk things out as they come up?' they ask. 'Why go to the bother of a formal set up - it sounds very stilted!' This is a valid objection, for it *is* important to practise problem-solving skills in our daily family life as issues crop up. But there is also great value in having formal meetings. After an initial reaction, children often become enthusiastic about them, get involved in discussions and decisions, and feel more committed to decisions made at this time. Recent surveys have shown that many young people would love to have the opportunity to express ideas in a calm atmosphere at home.

The idea of the family meeting is not to hand over decision-making to the children but to give them a real say in those decisions that affect their lives. Each one gets a chance to be heard, to ask questions, to make complaints, to offer suggestions. Together they can make plans and decisions, air grievances, agree on chores, solve problems - and the good that has been happening can be pointed out and encouraged.

That last point is important. Family meetings should not deal *merely* with problems and complaints. There should be time for encouragement and for planning treats, outings and fun. Otherwise, the meeting may lead to boredom and frustration.

Boredom will sometimes arise with matters that are important to one member of the family but of little concern to others. It may be better to deal with such matters on a one-to-one basis or in a smaller family grouping. For family meetings do not have to include the whole family - regular sit-down sessions with *individual* members of the family will often be easier and more helpful. The important thing is that we do not make decisions that affect the others without inviting them to take part in the discussion.

But why bother?

'Things are okay at present,' some parents will say. 'Leave well enough alone!' It is easy to forget that in family life a stitch in time really does save nine. It makes a lot of sense to take the time to deal with tensions and talk out limits in a relaxed, respectful way instead of constantly trying to cope with the crisis of the moment. Regular time spent talking out limits and 'rules' about bedtimes, chores, coming-in times, television, and so on, is time very well spent. In healthy families, limits are not established and sorted out once and for all - what is working well now may be much less effective in six months, or in a year. In the last chapter we saw that the key to good discipline is good communication, and these regular sit-down sessions, with one or more of the children at a time, are great for keeping the lines of communication open, establishing effective discipline, and fostering peaceful family living. They are marvellous for giving children the framework and limits they both fight against and crave. A half hour chat can turn chaos and depression into order and hope!

Helping to form values

There are many other advantages. James & Kathy McGinnis, authors of 'Parenting for Peace and Justice,' tell of a married couple they knew who opted for a simpler, more Christian life-style - but did not involve their children in that decision. The children reacted angrily to their parents' decision to buy second hand furniture, 'Why should we have to be poorer!' These children are now married and their values seem quite materialistic. James and Kathy, on the other hand, have been using family meetings for more than twelve years. In their family, some things are *not* open for discussion - like concern for the poor, recycling waste, simpler living - but they discuss and negotiate and compromise on the ways in which all this is done. The result is that their children do not seem to resent these things and have made these values their own. Involving them in making decisions enables them to learn to think for themselves, form sounder values and develop conscience.

How it works

Here are some general guidelines for family meetings.

It helps to meet at the same time every week - for a fixed time, perhaps 30-40 minutes (less for younger families). If possible, choose a time when those involved tend to be fairly relaxed and good-humoured (so not when a favourite television programme is on)!

It can help to begin meetings by looking over the decisions made at the last meeting - and to encourage any progress. Then, if you have not decided what is to be talked about, you can begin by asking what anyone *does* want to talk about, and write that down. Decide which topics you will take first, second, and so on, and ask for an agreement on these two guidelines, 1. 'No interrupting - wait until each person has finished speaking,' and 2. 'All agreements reached remain until the next family meeting.'

In dealing with each topic, the steps for solving problems can be followed, as in chapter five. First, people say how they see the problem. Next comes brainstorming - jotting down everyone's suggestions without any criticism. Then choosing one solution by looking together at the advantages and disadvantages of each suggestion. Finally, getting a commitment to the solution. It helps to write down any agreements made and to put the page up where everyone can be reminded of them.

Leading the meeting

Let's run quickly through a meeting then. The leader begins by looking at the decisions made at the previous meeting, 'How do you all feel about that now?' Next comes the first point on the 'agenda.' The person who wanted to talk about that point states the case and the leader asks, 'Anyone else like to say anything about this?' When everyone has had a chance to speak, one at a time, the question can be asked, 'Any ideas on how we might solve this problem?' When all suggestions have been made, each

one can be examined, 'How do you feel about solving it this way?' When a single solution begins to emerge, the leader can check, 'Is there general agreement on trying this?' And, 'Are we all willing to try it until the next meeting?'

Children tend to like all the trappings of chairperson, secretary, and agenda, and the formality can be good training for them, but words like these are not important - see what you are comfortable with. It is probably not a good idea to let one of the children lead the meeting until the parents have become skilled at doing so first. Parents can practise the skills and gain experience of running meetings for some time before beginning to involve the eldest child and later another, first as 'secretary' and then as leader. The 'secretary' makes a note of all decisions made.

Parents should not try to keep tight control on a meeting. They will obviously decide what is not for discussion, but they can encourage the children to be involved as much as possible in making suggestions and decisions. In general, it is best if parents encourage the *children* to make suggestions *first* on any given topic. In a two-parent family, father and mother might rotate as 'leader' and 'secretary.' The leader should:

1. Start and finish the meeting on time.
2. Keep people on one topic at a time.
3. Make sure everyone who wishes has a chance to speak on the topic.
4. Ask complainers what they think can be *done* about a problem.

Avoiding mistakes

The family meeting can be a good way to develop team-work and co-operation in a family. But the following mistakes can spoil the effect.

1. Not having a regular weekly time for meeting.
2. Starting late - or going on too long.
3. Having an emphasis on complaints and problems.
4. One parent not getting into the spirit of the meeting - or taking over.
5. Not keeping to agreements made.

Some of these mistakes will be made, of course, as a family learns the ropes. But the skills involved are soon learnt and there are many benefits. Family meetings quickly become part of a whole way of life.

How to begin family meetings.
An older family may be reluctant to have family meetings. If so, it may be necessary to use a family mealtime to deal with issues needing attention. That can gradually ease the family into more formal meetings. Generally, however, family meetings can be begun at any time - even with one child who is willing to give them a try. The children can be prepared by having the idea explained to them - they usually like the idea, but they can naturally be a little suspicious. Right from the start, they can be encouraged to say what they would like to talk about. It may also be helpful to *begin* family meetings by planning to discuss something that is interesting or *enjoyable* for the children.

Those who choose not to attend the meetings (including a father or mother) should not be forced to attend. But it is only fair to explain to them what will happen, for they may be affected by decisions made at meetings, for example about household chores. Sometimes, these same family members decide to join after a short time.

Children can be involved in family meetings from about age four. Meetings for young children, however, should only last for a short time, say twenty minutes, and need only deal with one topic per session. Instead of a family meeting, very young children can have a weekly 'family hour' - a time when parents make a special effort to chat and listen, to read stories, to play games and generally to build good memories for their children. Many parents of toddlers have found this time together to be invaluable, and it creates a good atmosphere in a home for starting family meetings at a later stage.

GETTING IN TOUCH

Parents used to make all the decisions in a home and children were very definitely expected to do what they were told. Today, some people think the shoe is on the other foot and that children have taken over in many homes. So what do **you** think?
1. Who do you think makes the decisions in the average home today - the parents? the children? both? For example, who decides how the children spend their time? Whose music is played in the living-room? How are the chores divided out and who decides? What other important decisions are made, and who makes them?
2. Who do you think *should* make the decisions?...

PLANS FOR NEXT WEEK

How might you introduce a regular family meeting - even with *one* of your children? What might be a suitable weekday/ time/ place? What will you say or do to make it attractive to your children? You may like to write down what you plan to do.

Plans..._____

TABLE 7: STAGES OF A FAMILY MEETING

1. Before the meeting. Find out what needs to be talked about. Perhaps attach a sheet of paper to the wall of the kitchen and allow anyone who wishes to add topics during the week.

2. The decisions we made. Some families like to begin with a short prayer. Next, look at the decisions made at the last meeting. 'How do we feel about them now?' Encourage any improvements or efforts. Make a note of what anyone is unhappy about - to talk over during the meeting.

3. Down to business. Take the first point to be talked about. 'Who wanted to speak about this?' Keep to the point and let anyone who wishes to speak have a turn. Show understanding and give each one a hearing. No arguing.

4. Brainstorming. Some points on the agenda are minor and can be dealt with very briefly. For important matters, gather ideas (brainstorm). 'Any ideas on what we might do for our outing?' No discussion or criticism of anyone's ideas at this stage - all suggestions should be noted.

5. Choosing a solution. Next, look at the suggestions. 'How do you feel about these ideas?' or 'Which of these suggestions do you like best?' If there is not general agreement, it may be necessary to postpone a decision until the following week - or try a temporary solution for one week.

6. Making a commitment. Once there is general agreement, get a commitment, 'Will we all try this until the next meeting?' This may include making arrangements about who does what, e.g., to prepare food, drinks and games for a family outing. (If someone later neglects to prepare, it may be best not to remind, thus allowing the family to learn from the consequence.)

7. One topic at a time. Deal with all major points in this way. Don't try to deal with many topics at one meeting, for it is important to stop at the time arranged - anything not talked about can be first for discussion next week.

8. Ending with a treat. It can be a good idea to have a special snack or treat to end the family meeting. That creates good memories and builds a stronger family bond. And some kind of family game suited to the ages and interests of the children can be an excellent follow-up to the meeting.

9. Putting decisions into action. Someone should be asked to make a note of the decisions made, and that can be put up on the wall of the kitchen as a useful reminder to all. This week's decisions can be talked about at the beginning of next week's meeting.

CASE STUDIES

(Alternative to listening to the audio tapes)

Read the following 'family meeting' (much better if four people read the four parts aloud). Then, in groups of three, see what skills you can pick out: encouragement, I-messages, brainstorming, active listening, etc. How do you feel about how the meeting is being run? - what is it that surprises you or seems different?

FATHER: Well, it's a week since our last meeting and I must say there's been a great improvement. It's nice to get up from the table and not to have to remind anyone about clearing up. So I think the decisions we made about the chores have helped. What about the rest of you? Are you happy with the decisions we made last week?

TIM: I'm not. Some people leave their plates on the table when they've finished, and Sheila takes so long eating that I have all the dishes washed by the time she's finished.

MOTHER: Yes, I noticed that. It makes it harder for you, Tim.

FATHER: Well, any suggestions about how we can solve this problem?

TIM: Sheila could finish her meal at the same time as the others.

SHEILA: Hey, that's not fair. I don't get home from school on time, so I'm late starting.

FATHER: Well, Tim has made one suggestion. Any others? (Pause)

TIM: I think if people forget to clear away their plates, they should wash them themselves.

SHEILA: That's terribly complicated. We'd end up arguing over who didn't clear their plates. I think it should be one person's chore to clear the table.

FATHER: Let me see now - that's three ideas - Sheila finish her meal with the others; wash your own dishes if you're late; or make clearing the table one person's chore. Any more?... (Silence). Well, Sheila's not happy with the first two ideas, so do you all think it would be a good idea to make clearing the table someone's chore?

TIM: . But whose chore would it be?

SHEILA: Why don't we swap around the chores? If I had to wash the dishes, I wouldn't be keeping anyone back.

FATHER: How would you feel about that, Tim? - if you came off wash-up and cleared the table instead.

TIM: Okay.

FATHER: Right, let's decide that until next week and we'll see how we get on... Now, what's the first point you all wanted to talk about?...

SHEILA: Mum wanted to talk about bedtimes.

MOTHER: Yes. I'm not happy about bedtimes. We agreed on ten o'clock for you, Sheila, and nine for you, Tim, but both times are being ignored evening after evening.

TIM: But Mom, nine o'clock is *far* too early. I can't even see the news!

SHEILA: He's right, Mum. Lots of girls in my class don't go to bed until after twelve.

MOTHER: I'm not talking about what other girls do. I just know that your father and I need a bit of time to *breathe* in the evenings, and I need you to respect that.

FATHER: That's important. Your mum and I need a bit of space at the end of the day. So how are we going to solve this?

SHEILA: Go to your room if you want time to breathe! Why should we have to suffer?

FATHER: That's one idea. Any others?

TIM: I wouldn't mind going to bed if I didn't have to put the lights out.

FATHER: Two suggestions. Any more? (Silence). So what does everyone think of the first suggestion - we go to our room.

MOTHER: You know that wouldn't work. There are lots of things to be done in the evenings. We just need peace and a chance to chat as we're doing them.

FATHER: And the second idea. Keep your bedtimes, but don't put the lights out?

MOTHER: No. I don't want you going about in the morning like zombies for want of sleep.

TIM: (Indignant). Mum, we're not babies!

SHEILA: Aw, come on, Mum!

MOTHER: Well, I don't mind you staying awake a bit later if we don't all have to pay the price for it with your grumpiness in the morning.

FATHER: Looks like the second solution is best then. But how will you work it so you won't be over-tired in the mornings?

TIM: Well, we could put the lights out after an hour.

MOTHER: An hour! No way. Let's see how things work out with half an hour first.

FATHER: But what I'd like to know is - are you going to take *responsibility* for switching off your lights without being *reminded*?

SHEILA: I am.

TIM: I am.

FATHER: Is that a promise - from both of you?

BOTH: Yes.

FATHER: Are you happy with that too, Christine?

MOTHER: Yes, I'll go along with it... But what happens if lights are not out on time?

FATHER: Okay - any ideas on what should happen if lights are not out on time?...

TIPS FOR PARENTS

When introducing new things into your family, it helps to start small and move slowly. No need to begin family meetings with a big commitment - better to start on the basis of 'Let's try a few family meetings and we'll see how they go. After the trial period, you can then see if the meetings can be established on a regular weekly basis.

It is important to give everyone the freedom not to attend meetings if they do not wish to attend. And if *everyone* is opposed to the idea you could bring up matters concerning the whole family over a meal instead. The others will not even realise that they are having a 'family meeting.' However, the formal setting is usually best.

It helps to begin meetings with a word of encouragement about any improvements or co-operation you may have noticed. Go out of your way to use encouragement and active listening during the meeting and to show respect for each suggestion. You can use I-messages to establish your own right to be respected, of course, but do keep a sense of humour!

It is suggested that you review the decisions taken at the previous meeting, write down any decisions made during the meeting and put them up where everyone can see them. That helps to make the decisions effective.

Use family meetings for enjoyable things like planning outings and treats as well as for dealing with problems.

At the end of each meeting it is good to ask yourself how you conducted the meeting, what skills you used effectively, and where you can improve next time.

For very young children a weekly 'family hour' can be very enjoyable - a special time for parents to play games, tell stories and generally have fun with their children. As time passes, this can gradually lead into a family meeting. But there should still be time for games, if possible, perhaps just after the meeting. This applies even when children are in their teens.

Meetings do not have to be formal - that depends on what suits your family. The important thing is that the family *does* meet - that each person has the opportunity to speak unhindered, and that they are given the respect of being listened to.

Family meetings do not have to be formal affairs - nor do they have to include the whole family. In fact, it can be helpful to have a regular sit-down session with at least *one* of the children - to talk through decisions that affect that child.

CHAPTER 8: BRINGING IT ALL TOGETHER

Twelve year old Sheila had been in a bad mood all morning. She greeted all questions with a grunt or a silent scowl. Eventually she had a run-in with her father and called him a pig. This was unacceptable behaviour, but her father, knowing that it was not the right time to deal with it effectively, refused to take the bait and did the opposite to what Sheila expected. 'Oink! oink.' he replied, playfully mimicking a pig.

It was not a bad approach. A sense of humour is a great help to a parent, and Sheila's father was able to take the heat out of a nasty situation by remembering that. For it is important to be flexible and human in applying the skills in this book.

That said, it is good to bear in mind that these skills can be helpful, not only for you as a parent, but also for your development as a person. They tend to spill over onto other relationships at work and in the community.

Settle for less than perfection.
We acquire skills when we practise using them regularly in all kinds of little ways. As with all skills - like learning to type, to play the guitar, etc. - you will appear at times to go backwards. That is natural. You often go backwards before taking a leap forward. So don't let yourself become discouraged.

Discouragement is a great enemy. It can be so easy to blame yourself and to think that you are responsible for your children's behaviour. You can be tempted to give up when everything does not go as planned. Your children may continue to keep their rooms untidy, to make mistakes, to test you in new ways. But your goal as a parent is not to achieve perfection. Your goal is to build better relationships with your children, to introduce more encouragement and more respect into your dealings with them, to change the atmosphere in your home, to help your children *begin* to grow into more responsible, co-operative, caring people.

So it can help when you settle for being less than perfect. We don't live in a perfect world. Some days we feel under the weather and find it hard to cope with anything. Sometimes we'll end up making decisions on the run, with no discussion -

'Look your bedtime is eight o'clock tonight - that's it!' Occasionally, we may end up letting bedtimes and chores and everything go by the board because we've too many other things to worry about. That's okay. It's not a life long pattern. It's no harm for your children to see you're human.

Let's look briefly over the main points of the course and try to bring them all together.

Becoming a responsible parent.

Underlying the whole course is the need to see all members of a family as equal.

Parents do have special responsibilities and a special leadership role, but each one in the family needs to be treated with respect - as a person of equal dignity. In the past, there was not enough respect for children; they were not equal. Today, it sometimes seems as if things have gone to the opposite extreme - too often it is the children who rule the parents. The balance may need to be restored. For we should not be slaves to our children, serving them and shielding them from their responsibilities. That is a misunderstanding of true love. The course encourages us to become *responsible* parents rather than 'good' parents.

It is clear, however, that this does not mean a return to the methods of the past. We do not have to decide what our children must wear, how they must behave, etc. That might produce the 'correct' behaviour while leaving the child immature, doing the right things for the wrong reasons. Children become responsible when they are given responsibility. So we need to allow them increasing freedom to choose. This will mean spending time with them, supporting them and training them to choose wisely. But when they do choose, we can allow them to live with the consequences of their choices - except in cases of real danger. In that way they will learn very quickly and we can have a big burden of discipline lifted off our shoulders.

It would seem to be important to keep a balance between letting go and continuing to be involved. It is not appropriate to hand over decision-making to children and expect them to make choices entirely on their own. They need our support and guidance as they gradually grow in their ability to make decisions. They need to hear what is important to us, what our beliefs are, what we like and dislike, what we value; they need our I-messages. Praise, as we have seen, may not be helpful, but they do need our encouragement - see if you can postpone corrections until later, and try to stop all criticism (*personal attack*). Keep on the look out for co-operation, efforts, and improvements to encourage. It helps to point to the good effects of what our children do without generalising or exaggerating. Perhaps more than anything else they need our *listening*, especially when they have problems or strong feelings. And they can constantly be learning from the example of our own lives.

The need for parents to change.

All that calls for change. It is hard to see how we can improve as parents until we are open to some change. Our children can begin to improve when we improve. And change is always possible.

We saw the value of this change in an early chapter. Children's 'misbehaviour' is usually a cry for attention, power, etc. As long as we continue to act as we have always acted, we may actually be *reinforcing* a child's behaviour. But when *we* make a positive change, a child will *also* tend to become more co-operative.

One of the big changes this course asks of us is to stop and think. When faced with a challenge, whether it be drugs, or under-age drinking, or just grumpiness and lack of co-operation, it is good to stop and ask ourselves, 'What is this child seeking?' or 'Who owns this problem - my child or me?' or 'How can I encourage this child to be more responsible in this situation?' These questions can open the way to dealing more effectively with a challenge.

To change ourselves is not easy. It often requires effort and *planning*. That is where a weekly family meeting can come in. Family meetings offer a unique opportunity to use and apply the skills of a responsible parent - listening, problem-solving, encouraging, giving responsibility, etc.

A balance also needs to be kept between these different skills, however. Some parents who do this course become good at withdrawing from conflict and using consequences. Their improvement is very real and heartening. If, however, this skill is emphasised at the expense of listening and encouraging, the children may end up feeling frustrated. They may experience the use of consequences as punishment. So it is good to be flexible, to err on the side of affection and to try to practise using encouragement and listening every day. They are probably the two most important skills a parent can have.

Determination to keep improving.

Finally, a word about where you might like to go from here. Some parents actually like to do this course a number of times, but there is no substitute for the effort to apply the skills. That requires determination and is difficult without the support of others who have done a course like this. Some kind of support group can make all the difference.

A great deal is at stake. Many of us tend to drift along, not asking ourselves what we really want in life. Perhaps we want to have a good time, interesting work, money... But what of that special task entrusted to every parent? To number our children among our best friends. To be effective, loving parents - caring, open, responsible and encouraging. To support our children as they develop and grow into caring, responsible adults, capable of playing their part in improving the society we live in and making our world more just and peaceful. It is unlikely that anything could ever bring us as much happiness and fulfilment.

GETTING IN TOUCH

1. Have a look at the last column of Table 8 - the responsible approach. Can you find examples there of the following skills? - applying consequences; offering choices; developing responsibility; encouragement; active listening; brainstorming; giving I-messages; withdrawing; using the four stages of problem-solving.

2. Now take a look at the *first* column of Table 8. Which approach (dictator or permissive) do *you* tend to take when you meet challenges like these? Does the 'responsible approach' column help you to see how you might be able to change your approach?

3. Could you add a ninth problem/challenge to the first column? - perhaps one that you meet from your own child. How might you fill in the other columns to match it?

PLANNING AHEAD

1. What single change would you most like to introduce into your family over the next few months? What plans do you need to make to introduce it? What will help you to remember that? You may like to write down your plan.

2. How about sitting down on your own at a specific time each weekend and thinking, 'What is causing tension or unpleasantness in the family?' What might improve this? When can I talk it out with the child(ren)?'

Plans..._____

_____

TABLE 8: THE RESPONSIBLE APPROACH

Table 8 shows three different approaches parents can take. Those who take the responsible approach can meet a challenge by asking themselves, 'Who owns this problem?' 'What is this child's goal?' or 'How can I encourage responsibility here?'

Problem Behaviour/ Challenge	Dictator Approach	Permissive Approach	Responsible Approach
1. Child refuses to eat.	Lecture, force, or scold.	Allow child to have own way.	Begin to involve child in planning meals. Use consequences, e.g. 'no dessert if dinner is not eaten.'
2. Child not working at school.	Stand over child, force, punish, nag.	Bribe - or ignore completely.	Allow child to take responsibility for own school work, but show interest and encourage improvement/ effort.
3. Child defies parent/ is disobedient.	Threaten. Force.	Coax, apologise, or plead.	Don't correct on the spot. Perhaps use active listening. Postpone discussion until child is calmer.
4. Child 'forgets' chores.	Remind, scold, demand, nag.	Do the chores yourself.	Mention it at family meeting and brainstorm on consequences of neglecting chores
5. Child rude to parents in front of visitors.	Make scene, order, humiliate.	Pretend not to notice, plead, bribe.	Give child choice. Give I-message when friends leave.
6. Child breaks a window.	Lose temper, humiliate, shout.	Fix window. 'It doesn't matter.'	Stay calm. Ask child (if old enough) to pick up glass. Make arrangements to subtract cost from pocket money.
7. Teenage child refuses to go to church.	Make scene, threaten, insist.	Remind, plead, coax - or just say nothing.	Postpone discussion. Later, use four stages of problem-solving, including listening and speaking your own values.
8. Child hit by older sister.	Judge. Scold. Punish older sister.	Console, 'Don't cry.' Ask not to hit.	Use active listening, but allow child to settle own fights, when possible.
9. A challenge you meet in your own family.			

CASE STUDIES

(Alternative to listening to the audio tapes)

Read the following conversations (it may be better if two or three people read them aloud). Then, in groups of three, discuss the questions at the end of each situation.

MOTHER: They're your good shoes, Jim - you know you can't go out in the mud in them.
JIM: Aw, mum, the boys are waiting. You always spoil my fun.
DAD: I can't see why he can't go out in those shoes. They'll do okay. Let him run on.
MOTHER: Well, I'm the one who has to clean the mud off the carpet when he doesn't change. Are you prepared to do that if he comes back in with muddy shoes?
DAD: Oh, okay.

What usually happens in a case like this? What skills is the mother using? What do you think of her approach?

Five year old Catherine has scarcely touched her dinner, but wants to have her pudding. Her father explains that she doesn't have to eat her dinner if she doesn't want to, but she can't have pudding if she doesn't eat it. Granny has been listening, and now interrupts:
GRANNY: Of course the child can have her pudding, Gerry. I didn't starve you when you were a child. Here's your pudding, dear - and just enjoy it.... I never heard such nonsense!
FATHER: I appreciate your kindness to Catherine, Mom. But I really don't want her to develop bad eating habits, and I feel upset and discouraged when you give in to her like this.

What usually happens in a situation like this? What skills is the father using? He may not get granny to change, of course, but what are the advantages of this approach?

Every morning Mr. Walsh used to shout, nag, and scold to get his fifteen year old daughter, Sandra, out to school. Since doing this course, however, Mr. Walsh is encouraging Sandra to take more responsibility for herself in the mornings. The result is that Sandra is often late for school. Mr. Walsh believes that she should face the consequences of being late, but one evening Sandra's teacher happens to meet Mr. Walsh.
TEACHER: Oh, Mr. Walsh, could I have a word with you? It's about Sandra. I'm sorry to have to tell you she's been late to school almost every day for the past two weeks. I wonder could you make sure she gets in on time in future.
MR WALSH: Thank you for mentioning this. That must be very annoying for you to have Sandra come in late when you're trying to get things done.
TEACHER: It certainly is. You'll have to do something about it.
MR WALSH: Have you spoken to Sandra about this yourself?
TEACHER: Oh yes. But it doesn't seem to have made any difference.
MR WALSH: I see. That makes it more difficult, doesn't it. And what do you usually do with a child who doesn't behave?
TEACHER: Well, I sometimes speak to the parents... Or I send her to the principal.
MR WALSH: Well, thanks for speaking to me, Miss Wright: I've told Sandra I want her to take responsibility for getting to school on time, and I want you to feel perfectly free to deal with her in the usual way. It might do her no harm to have to face the principal.

What usually happens in a case like this? What skills is Mr. Walsh using? How do you feel about his approach?

TIPS FOR PARENTS

Try the 'little and often' approach to learning new skills. It might be a good idea, for example, to read back over a chapter of this book at a definite time each week and to decide (preferably with a partner) what skill you will try to practise that week, who with, and when. That can bring about real change.

Don't aim too high. Parents who settle for a good deal less than perfection save themselves a lot of frustration and discouragement.

It helps to look at the bright side, to see problems as challenges and not to listen to discouragement. Remember - change is always possible.

When faced with misbehaviour, do your best not to react on the spot. Better to stop and ask yourself a few questions, 'Who owns this problem?'; 'What is this child seeking?'; 'How can I encourage this child to be more responsible?' You might like to try asking yourself those questions about some problem you have with a child right now. The more you practise doing that, the quicker your approach can change.

The reason why most parents do not change is because they drift along without planning or reflecting, reacting as they have always reacted. Consider taking a little quiet time for reflection and planning each day. You might think about your family and how each one is growing in responsibility.

Helping children to be co-operative and responsible takes time - *your* time. That is the biggest change that is being asked of you - to spend time enjoying your children, encouraging them, listening to them. Encouraging and listening are probably the two most important skills a parent can have.

It is difficult to go it alone. Most people seem to need to give and receive support. You may like to keep in touch on a fairly regular basis with some of the people who have done the course with you.

This book does not deal directly with children's moral development, but you are obviously laying an excellent foundation for their moral development when you help them to make responsible decisions.

There is no instant recipe for bringing up children. Different children, different situations, different circumstances, all call for different approaches on the part of a parent. For example, if applying consequences only gets a child's back up and does not appear to be working in a particular instance, then drop it and try something else - perhaps more encouragement. If encouragement is genuine, children can never get too much of it.

COMMENTS FROM OTHER PARENTS

The comments below were all made by parents following the "Fives to Fifteens" Parenting Programme.

When I stopped interfering in the fights, the children couldn't cope with me and the screaming actually got worse for a while, they were so desperate to draw me into it all. But that's one of things I've got out of this course - to ignore the squabbles. I was wearing myself out being the judge, asking who hit who first and who said what, and why did she do that, and so on. Now I realise they had become past masters at getting my attention with their screams and tattling on one another. I just tell them I trust them to sort it out themselves now and it works most of the time.

My daughter looked at me in amazement and said 'Mummy, what's wrong? You don't shout at me any more.

A few years ago, I heard of a father who spends every Saturday morning with his children, one of them at a time, doing whatever the child wants him to do. I thought it was such a good idea that I started it myself. Since then, I've done some of the craziest things with my children - I've cycled, explored, played football, had picnics and walks, even put up birds' nests in the trees! But it has built a great bond with them and I've given them memories that will last, I'm sure, until they die.

I was a smother-mother all these years, lifting and laying them, waiting on them hand and foot. Now I see I was only training them to grow up expecting others to serve them. What kind of marriages would they make with that attitude!

I have involved my son in clearing up after meals and we've had some great chats together as he washes and I dry. There is something about working together without facing each other that makes it easier to talk about difficult things.

As I listened to the examples I kept saying: 'That's me!' I scold and give out and find fault all day long. To tell you the truth, I wouldn't like to live in a house with a person like me.

When I asked Maurice to cut the grass, he said: 'You expect me to be your slave and do everything around here! Anyway, I can't work that push mower!' I said: 'Maurice, I'd be glad if you would do it, but you don't have to. In fact, two weeks ago the grass was quite long and I was surprised that you made such a clean job of it. So you've already done more than your fair share.' Then I left him. A few minutes later he was out working like a Trojan at the grass. The few words of encouragement had worked.

She was surprised I could understand. She felt an adult couldn't possibly know what a thirteen year old girl was going through. She told me that. And it seemed as if the gap between us began to close.

I've started taking time to ask questions and listen to their little stories. It's so right.'

'Active listening' sounds totally unnatural to me. I mean, people just don't talk like that. My children would think something was wrong with me. They would tell me I needed to go and get my head examined.

I like the emphasis on listening. When I've listened well, I've seen Tom change from being depressed and hopeless about things. He didn't need me to tell him what to do - he was able to work it out for himself.

She knew she was in the wrong and she was bristling as she got ready for my usual attack. Instead, I said, 'Janet, when you stay out so late, I feel frightened and scared in case something has happened to you.' It was a more civilised approach, and you could see her softening.

I find a good way to break the deadlock is to give them a choice - if you don't decide quickly, I'll decide for you.

Using consequences did harm to my relationship with John. It made me a bit cold and removed as a parent - and he saw consequences as punishment. I think you have to be careful about how you introduce consequences with a teenager. It helps me to ask myself, 'Is this really going to make him more responsible?

You can't just tell children to sort out their own squabbles, and then go off and leave them there. You sometimes need to spend time with them helping them to see how differences can be settled without hitting or kicking or saying hurtful things.

It sounds very forced. I mean, good God, what kind of a family needs to have a chairperson and a secretary? There's a lot of good in this course and I've learnt a lot of things, but this idea of having a sort of business meeting has no place in a family.

The first few family meetings were disastrous. Nobody seemed to want to co-operate and I ended up arguing and scolding. It was when I started using the four stages of problem-solving that things improved. Children need limitations and guidelines and, when they have no framework, there's chaos.

The little boy in the house next to me was driving his mother around the bend. As a result of the course she took control and I saw a transformation in him. That's what made me do the course.

What I appreciated about the course was the sense of support from others. It helped me to realise that we are all in the same boat. And that other parents are making the same mistakes as myself. It doesn't seem so hard when you're not alone.

This course has been my lifesaver. I feel more capable of dealing with the children now. I don't blow my top as much, I boss less and we're better friends. I just wish I had done it years ago'.

I used to think that all a parent needed was love. Love was the answer. The course has helped me to see that you need *skills* as well. You *know* you need skills for nursing or teaching and so on - that love isn't enough - yet you drift into being a parent without any training whatsoever.

'To say that the course has changed our family life is an understatement. Thank you for liberating me from what seemed like a prison - rearing my children with no tools and poor skills.

CHILDREN HAVE NEEDS...

If children live with criticism they learn to condemn.
If children live with hostility they learn to fight.
If children live with ridicule they learn to be shy.
If children live with shame they learn to feel guilty.
If children live with tolerance they learn to be patient.
If children live with encouragement they learn confidence.
If children live with appreciation they learn to appreciate.
If children live with fairness they learn justice.
If children live with security they learn to have faith.
If children live with approval they learn to like themselves.
If children live with acceptance and friendship they learn to find love.

...AND MORE NEEDS

Don't spoil me. I know quite well I ought not to have all I ask for. I'm only testing you.
Don't be afraid to be firm with me. I prefer it. It makes me feel more secure.
Don't let me form bad habits. I need you to detect them at early stages.
Don't correct me in front of people if you can help it. I'll take more notice if you talk quietly with me in private.
Don't make me feel my mistakes are sins. It upsets my sense of values.
Don't protect me from consequences. I need to learn the painful way sometimes.
Don't be too upset when I say 'I hate you.' I say it when I hate myself.
Don't take too much notice of my small ailments. Sometimes they get the attention I need.
Don't nag. If you do, I'll have to protect myself by appearing deaf.
Don't forget that I can't explain myself as well as I'd like to. That is why I am not always very accurate.
Don't make rash promises. I feel let down when promises are broken.
Don't tax my honesty too much. I'm easily frightened into telling lies.
Don't tell me my fears are silly. They're terribly real - and you can help if you try to understand.
Don't put me off when I ask questions. If you do, you'll find that I stop asking and seek my information elsewhere.
Don't ever think it's beneath your dignity to apologise to me. An honest apology makes me feel surprisingly warm towards you.
Don't ever suggest that you're perfect or infallible. It gives me too great a shock when I discover you're neither.
Don't forget I love experimenting. I couldn't get on without it. So please put up with it.
Don't forget I can't thrive without lots of understanding love.

FURTHER READING

*In writing this book, we have attempted to produce something short, simple and practical. For those who want more, there are many good books on parenting. Here are just a few. Some of them, perhaps, take too rigid, or too democratic an approach. The authors prefer to see more emphasis on parental affection, example and guidance, with a **gradual** handing over of responsibilities to a child. That said, there is a great deal to recommend in these books. (See also the books from Family Caring Trust on pages 70-71.)*

The Parent's Handbook, by Don Dinkmeyer and Gary McKay. Many ideas in 'What can a parent do?' are more fully developed in this colourful book. Publ AGS, Circle Pines, Minnesota.

Happy Children, by Rudolf Dreikurs. Helpful on how parents can allow younger children learn from the consequences of their behaviour. Good examples. Publ. Collins/Fontana.

Parent Effectiveness Training, by Dr Thomas Gordon. A classic book for parents that is particularly good on active listening, I-messages, and problem solving. Publ. Plume Books.

The Magic of Encouragement, by Stephanie Marston. Excellent on what many consider the most important skill of all. Publ. Simon and Schuster, Inc.

The Parents Book, by Ivan Sokolov and Deborah Hutton. An understanding book, coming out of the experience of parents in the Parent Network support groups. Publ. Thorsons.

The New Peoplemaking, by Virginia Satir. An interesting book for parents who wish to understand what is happening between family members. Offers hope for changing destructive family patterns. Publ. Science and Behaviour Books, California, 1988.

A Family Meeting Handbook, by Robert Slagle. A practical book with good examples, although the vocabulary could be simpler for the average parent. Publ Family Relations Foundation, Sebastopol, CA 95472, USA.

Parenting for Peace and Justice, by James and Kathy McGinnis. Looks at how parents can help develop concern for the poor and for justice issues within the family. Published Orbis, New York

The Parent's Guide, by Don Dinkmeyer and Gary McKay. Looks at the special challenges provided by teenagers. Well argued and clearly presented. Publ AGS, Circle Pines Minnesota.

Two books to help you understand families and current thinking about the family are:

Families and how to survive them, by Robin Skynner and John Cleese. Publ. Methuen

The Family: A revolutionary way of self-discovery, by John Bradshaw. Publ. Health Communications, Florida.

APPENDIX: A SPIRITUAL DIMENSION

People who have religious faith can usually draw strength from their religious tradition in improving their parenting skills and in seeing their parenting as an opportunity to share in God's creative work. This can give added meaning to their lives as parents. The ideas in this programme, so far from being in conflict with religious beliefs, are usually rooted in a deeper understanding of these very traditions. Some of the reflections in this section may help to bring that out.

Chapter 1: Towards the end of chapter one, there is considerable emphasis on the need for time together. This time together (including, perhaps, time for family prayer), lays the foundation on which a good home atmosphere can be built. It is also a vital foundation for the growth of children's faith. Their experience of a loving parent can be an important starting-point for their experience of a loving God, for children's images of God are formed early in life and are usually closely linked to how they see their parents.

Chapter 2: We have just seen that children learn how much God cares for them from their experience of how their parents care for them. So we give children a false image of God if we become their doormats and do not encourage them to take on responsibilities. God parents all of us by giving us great freedom to make our own decisions and by allowing us to live with the consequences - at the same time loving and supporting us in more ways than we can imagine.

Chapter 3: In Chapter Three it is suggested that encouragement needs to come from the heart - from a genuine appreciation of our children's goodness - and that many people are helped by a regular period of meditation, reflection or personal prayer which makes them aware of God's goodness in themselves and in others. For it is difficult to love and to encourage until we experience being loved and encouraged ourselves.

Chapter 4: We are told in this chapter that listening is much more than a mere technique or skill; it is one of the most effective ways of expressing love. St Paul highlights active listening when he encourages us to 'rejoice with those who rejoice and weep with those who weep.'

Chapter 5: Many of the traditional ways in which parents dealt with problems did not show respect for children, so it is important to find peaceful, respectful ways of dealing with anger and conflict, as in this chapter. Working for justice and peace in a family is clearly central to a parent's spirituality. This can also include asking forgiveness of children, which is now a feature of family prayer in some homes.

Chapter 6: This chapter develops further the peaceful, non-violent methods of the previous chapter by providing an alternative to traditional methods of disciplining children by force. We are reminded that 'love does not insist on its own way.'

Chapter 7: The family meeting is an important way of realising the Christian vision of family life, 'Submit yourselves to one another because of your reverence for Christ...Children, obey your parents... Parents, do not treat your children in such a way as to make them angry.'

Chapter 8: The skills in this entire course are central to the holiness and spirituality of a parent, for the call to love one another obviously applies especially to those in our own family. Indeed, a weekly review of progress, some planning for the following week, and regular prayer that is directed to developing responsibility in our children and improving as a parent can form a sound basis for a very practical spirituality for parents.

MAKING AGREEMENTS

At the beginning of a course, it may help to discuss and agree on the following guidelines and any other points parents wish to raise.

1. Take it seriously. People generally find this course enjoyable, but you are also asked to take it seriously. It is important, for example, to come to all eight meetings and to practise the skills in between sessions, for each session builds on the one before it. Those who work hard at the skills between sessions tend to see a great improvement in themselves and in their children.

2. Play your part. Some people are naturally shy and reluctant to speak, even in a small group. No one at any stage *has* to talk in the group, but talking things out together can help both you and the others, so the more open you can be the better.

3. Give the others a chance. This guideline is for the person who tends to talk too much. Please don't speak a second time about a topic until everyone has at least had an opportunity to speak once. Hogging the conversation is just not fair to the others. If you tend to overtalk, try going out of your way to draw others out and to encourage them to talk first.

4. Respect people's confidences: During the course, it may happen that members of the group will trust you by telling you personal things about their children. If so, it is important to respect that trust and not to talk about such matters outside the group, because things can sound quite different when they are spoken about out of context.

5. Take it slowly. Don't let discouragement beat you if you make mistakes or seem to be slow about getting results. Learning new skills takes time and patience - you know what it's like learning to cook, to ride a bike, to type, or to play a musical instrument. 'Little and often' is the golden rule for picking up new skills - taking on only a little at a time but practising it often.

6. What works for you. You're not expected to use or to agree with everything on this course. Many parents are already doing a very good job and are not using all these methods - we're all different. But you are asked to give new ideas a fair chance by trying them out - that's the only way to find out what *might* work for you.

7. What works for others. We have just seen that you have a right to be different. You are asked to respect that difference in *others* too. People have a right to their own approach and their own opinion. What works for you may not work for them, so do share with others what works for you, but please do not offer them advice - it is just not helpful to tell others in the group what you think *they* ought to do. In the same spirit of respect, the group leaders will not offer advice either.

8. Look out for strengths. Please do not use the group to make little of your children or to criticise others. Keep on the look-out for strengths and improvements, for this is a positive, family-building support group. It is also a basic principle of the course that to be effective I need to begin by changing *myself*; my children will begin to change when I do.

9. Don't tell me - show me. It is not helpful to lecture others or to try to convert them to your new methods. This applies especially to partners if they are not doing the course with you. The best way to convince anyone about something is to show by your example that it works.

SUPPORT FOR PARENTING

THE NOUGHTS TO SIXES PARENTING PROGRAMME

Seven or eight weekly sessions offering effective parenting support to parents of babies, toddlers, pre-schoolers and children in the first few years of primary school. Simply written, jargon-free, common sense approach. Produced in co-operation with Barnardos. The boxed kit includes a video (incorporating the BBC's acclaimed QED programme on parenting), two leader's guides, twenty-five certificates, and one copy of the parent's handbook, **From Pram to Primary School.**

THE FIVES TO FIFTEENS BASIC PARENTING PROGRAMME

Eight weekly sessions to help parents of children five to fifteen years old to improve their communication skills and create a framework of discipline and respect in their families. It is the Trust's most popular programme. The boxed kit includes a video (about 10 mins input for each session), 2 leader's guides, 25 certificates, and one copy of the parent's handbook, **What Can A Parent Do?**

THE TEEN PARENTING PROGRAMME

Six weekly sessions to reinforce the same skills as the basic parenting programme while dealing with the more difficult situations met in the teen years. Because it is so important to reinforce skills being learnt, it is recommended, but not essential, that parents of teenagers experience the Fives to Fifteens programme first. The kit includes 3 cassette tapes, 6 posters, 2 leader's guides, 25 certs, and one copy of the parent's handbook, **What Can The Parent Of A Teenager Do?**

THE PARENT ASSERTIVENESS PROGRAMME

Seven weekly sessions learning basic assertive skills applied to the workplace or neighbourhood, but especially to family situations. A good way of complementing what has been learnt in the other parenting programmes. Produced in co-operation with Barnardos. The boxed kit includes 2 leader's guides, a video cassette, and one copy of the participant's handbook, **Being Assertive.**

THE PARENTING AND SEX PROGRAMME

Five weekly sessions to help parents learn skills for talking, and getting children talking, about sex (parents are often overlooked in the sex-education process that targets schools and youth clubs). Preferably for parents of primary school children, but it also looks at areas like dating, television viewing, peer pressure... The kit consists of a leader's guide and one copy of the parent's handbook, **Parenting and Sex.**

SUPPORT FOR YOUNG ADULTS

THE YOUNG ADULT ASSERTIVENESS PROGRAMME

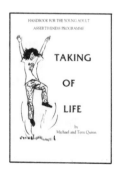

Eight weekly sessions to help young adults, 15 or 16 upwards, learn the same respectful skills as their parents and thus reinforce change within the family system. The emphasis is on saying "no" to peer pressure, growth in self-confidence, and finding fairer, less aggressive ways of dealing with problems. The boxed kit includes a video, 2 leader's guides, a pack of 25 certs, and one copy of the participant's handbook, **Taking Charge of your Life.**

SUPPORT FOR COUPLES

THE "GROWING IN LOVE" PROGRAMME

Four weekly sessions for groups of women *without* their partners. One encouraging effect is that many men (who have not attended a course) are so pleased with the *effects* that they become open to experiencing a course for couples (also provided for in the kit). The boxed kit includes 2 cassette tapes, 2 leader's guides (one for running single-sex groups, and one for running groups of couples), and one copy of the participant's handbook, **Growing in Love.**

THE "COUPLE ALIVE" PROGRAMME

Six weekly sessions for couples at all stages - engaged, cohabiting, recently married or married up to forty years. Helps couples deepen or renew their love, commitment and understanding for one another. Also teaches the "Listen and Check" method which has dramatically reduced rates of separation, divorce and domestic violence among couples who have learned to use it in Europe and the United States. The boxed kit includes a video, 2 leader's guides, and a participant's handbook, **Couple Alive.**

AND FOR CHURCHES...

THE "ENJOY PRAYING" PROGRAMME

Six weekly sessions, often as a follow-up to a parenting programme, to introduce people to a variety of ways of praying with scripture so that they can choose what suits them best. There is emphasis on family spirituality. Produced in co-operation with the mainstream Christian churches. The kit consists of a leader's guide and a participant's handbook, **Enjoy Praying.**

There is also an *optional* religious dimension (Christian or Islamic) in each of the Trust's courses.

ADDITIONAL RESOURCES

Introductory video 25-min. video cassette useful for information evening/introductory session. Shows effect of parenting course on two families. Made independently by RTE, and provided at duplication cost.
Leader's tape. Audio tape to help facilitators understand their role and reinforce some skills they need.
The Family Dinner Game. A game for younger (pre-teen) families. Nurtures communication, fun and emotional support - all over a family meal around the table.
Stepfamilies Programme Facilitator's Guide and Parent's Handbook for 8-session course exploring situations facing step-parents and offering them helpful skills for building and strengthening their families. Developed and tested by the National Stepfamilies Association.

More than a quarter of a million parents have experienced the Trust's courses to date. In addition to being widely used by social services, and by well over a thousand schools and adult education bodies, the Trust's programmes have been adopted or endorsed by the following organisations:

**The Health Visitors' Association Barnardos NCH The Children's Society
Homestart All the mainstream Christian Churches NSPCC Mothers' Union
The Psychological Services in Scotland. The Marriage Enrichment Association.**

Barnardos and the Dept of Health have also contributed to the development and production of some of the Trust's programmes, and the basic parenting programme has been translated into Welsh by the Children's Society.

The Family Listening Game

If you appreciated your parenting course, here's an enjoyable, easy way to build on it for the future. You can continue to develop the parenting skills you have been learning with a game developed by the same authors to make family mealtimes more lively and interesting. Here are some of the things you can do with it:

- **Enjoy laughter, intimacy and great conversations around the table.**
- **Discover your own unsuspected gifts as a conversationalist.**
- **Help your children's social and emotional development.**
- **Have fun playing a non-competitive game.**
- **Get to know your children as never before.**
- **Build lasting memories for all the family.**
- **Give everyone at the table a sense of being "heard."**
- **Assist your children in forming enduring values.**
- **And help to start a new fashion that offers an alternative to the TV culture and the poor family communications that often result.**
- **(Or give it as a gift to a family you appreciate.)**

A gift to a family at only £14.80 (includes Vat, postage and packing)

- -

Please send me *The Family Listening Game* (from 30 Oct. 1996). I enclose cheque/ P.O for £14.80.

NAME (BLOCK LETTERS PLEASE) _____

ADDRESS _____

_____ Post Code_____